"Authored by a team of inter~~n~~
research has shaped many of
sexuality studies, *Objectificatio~~n~~*
to consider the subtle differenc~~e~~
and objectification arguing that
lap, they are not the same thing. Addressing topics ranging from
selfie culture to contemporary trans rights, *Objectification* makes a
timely intervention into media and cultural studies. Written in an
accessible style, which is free from academic jargon, this book will
be important reading for both academic researchers and students
who are new to the subject area."

Niall Richardson, Convenor of MA Gender and Media,
University of Sussex, UK

Objectification

This is a concise and accessible introduction into the concept of objectification, one of the most frequently recurring terms in both academic and media debates on the gendered politics of contemporary culture, and core to critiquing the social positions of sex and sexism.

Objectification is an issue of media representation and everyday experiences alike. Central to theories of film spectatorship, beauty fashion and sex, objectification is connected to the harassment and discrimination of women, to the sexualization of culture and the pressing presence of body norms within media. This concise guidebook traces the history of the term's emergence and its use in a variety of contexts such as debates about sexualization and the male gaze, and its mobilization in connection with the body, selfies and pornography, as well as in feminist activism.

It will be an essential introduction for undergraduate and postgraduate students in Gender Studies, Media Studies, Sociology, Cultural Studies or Visual Arts.

Susanna Paasonen is Professor of Media Studies at University of Turku, Finland. With an interest in studies of sexuality, networked media and affect, she is the Principal Investigator of both the Academy of Finland research project, "Sexuality and Play in Media Culture" and the Strategic Research Council funded consortium, "Intimacy in Data-Driven Culture". Examples of her publications include *Who's Laughing Now? Feminist Tactics in Social Media* (MITP, forthcoming, with Jenny Sundén), *NSFW: Sex, Humor and Risk in Social Media* (MITP, 2019, with Kylie Jarrett and Ben Light),

Many Splendored Things: Thinking Sex and Play (Goldsmiths Press, 2018) and *Carnal Resonance: Affect and Online Pornography* (MITP, 2011).

Feona Attwood is the co-editor of *Sexualities* and founding co-editor of *Porn Studies*. Her research focuses on the changing place and significance of gender and sex and their representation in contemporary society. It examines the ways in which sexual practices and representations are caught up in wider debates around bodies, media and technologies, and the emerging centrality of new technologies in conceptions of gender and sexuality. She is the author of *Sex Media* (Wiley, 2018), co-editor of *The Routledge Companion to Media, Sex and Sexuality* (Routledge, 2017) and *Controversial Images: Media Representations on the Edge* (Palgrave Macmillan, 2012) and editor of *Mainstreaming Sex: The Sexualization of Western Culture* (I.B. Tauris, 2009).

Alan McKee is an expert on entertainment and healthy sexual development. He holds an Australian Research Council Discovery grant entitled "Pornography's Effects on Audiences: Explaining Contradictory Research Data". He recently completed a Wellcome Grant entitled "Investigating Mediated Sex and Young People's Health and Well-being" and an ARC Linkage grant with True (previously Family Planning Queensland) to investigate the use of vulgar comedy to provide information about healthy sexual development to young men. He was co-editor of the *Girlfriend Guide to Life* and co-author of *Pornography: Structures Agency and Performance* (Polity, 2015). He has published on healthy sexual development, and entertainment education for healthy sexuality in journals, including the *Archives of Sexual Behavior*, the *International Journal of Sexual Health*, the *Journal of Sex Research* and *Sex Education*.

John Mercer is Professor of Gender and Sexuality at Birmingham City University. He is the Principal Investigator (with Clarissa Smith) of the "Masculinity, Sex and Popular Culture" AHRC research network and is co-editor with Clarissa Smith of the Routledge book series of the same name. He is the author of *Gay Porn: Representations of Masculinity and Sexuality* (I.B. Tauris, 2017), *Rock Hudson* (BFI Publishing, 2015) and of *Melodrama: Genre*

Style Sensibility (with Martin Shingler) (Columbia University Press, 2004). He is co-editor of the *Journal of Gender Studies, Porn Studies*, and editorial board member of *Sexualities* and *Celebrity Studies*. He has written about film and television genres, celebrity and stardom, the pornography debate, the sexualization of contemporary media culture and contemporary masculinity. His research interests concern the politics of representation, in particular sexual representation, the connections between gay pornography and the making of a gay identity, the social and cultural construction of masculinities, performances of gender in the media and the wider culture, and melodrama, emotion and affect in the media and their gendered modes of address.

Clarissa Smith is Professor in the Media School at Northumbria University. A founding co-editor of *Porn Studies*, Clarissa's research is focused on representations of sex and sexuality, their production and consumption. Publications include numerous articles and chapters exploring the specificities of pornographic imagery, forms of stardom, production and regulation. She is interested in media consumption and how different audiences engage with and make sense of popular representations; she is also engaged in research to explore young people's practices of digital self-representation and participation.

Gender Insights

https://www.routledge.com/Gender-Insights/book-series/GendIn

Objectification

On the Difference between Sex and Sexism

Susanna Paasonen, Feona Attwood, Alan McKee, John Mercer and Clarissa Smith

Routledge
Taylor & Francis Group

LONDON AND NEW YORK

First published 2021
by Routledge
2 Park Square, Milton Park, Abingdon, Oxon OX14 4RN

and by Routledge
52 Vanderbilt Avenue, New York, NY 10017

*Routledge is an imprint of the Taylor & Francis Group, an
informa business*

British Library Cataloguing-in-Publication Data
A catalogue record for this book is available from the British
Library

Library of Congress Cataloging-in-Publication Data
Names: Attwood, Feona, author.
Title: Objectification : on the difference between sex and sexism /
Feona Attwood [and four others].
Description: Abingdon, Oxon ; New York, NY : Routledge, 2020. |
Series: Gender insights | Includes bibliographical
references and index. |
Identifiers: LCCN 2020014803 (print) | LCCN 2020014804 (ebook) |
ISBN 9780367199098 (hardback) | ISBN 9780367199111 (paperback)
| ISBN 9780429244032 (ebook) | ISBN 9780429520778 (adobe pdf) |
ISBN 9780429534249 (epub) | ISBN 9780429548949 (mobi)
Subjects: LCSH: Sex role. | Objectification (Social psychology) |
Sex | Sexism.
Classification: LCC HQ1075 .A886 2020 (print) | LCC HQ1075
(ebook) | DDC 305.3--dc23
LC record available at https://lccn.loc.gov/2020014803
LC ebook record available at https://lccn.loc.gov/2020014804

ISBN: 978-0-367-19909-8 (hbk)
ISBN: 978-0-367-19911-1 (pbk)
ISBN: 978-0-429-24403-2 (ebk)

Typeset in Sabon
by Taylor & Francis Books

Contents

Figures

1 What counts as objectification?

Kim Kardashian-West is currently one of the most famous women on the planet, and one of the things she is most famous for is objectifying herself (see Figure 1.1). Kardashian has created a massive public archive of images documenting almost every aspect of her everyday life, from professionally-taken glamour shots to seemingly casual selfies shared with some 153 million followers on her Instagram account. Many of those images show off her body, revealing its contours in little or no clothing and modelled in sexy poses. Kardashian's rise to fame was fuelled by the reality TV show *Keeping Up with the Kardashians* (2007–) focusing on her family after a sex tape, released by her then boyfriend in 2007, became the most watched adult video of all time, gaining 150 million online views during its first decade alone. Critics abound. "She has successfully reduced herself to one thing ... a vapid sex object" (Khona 2016: np), they say, presenting to the world her "disempowered 'I am a sex object' pose" (Mollard, 2016: np). Critics ask her how she feels about "objectifying herself with selfies" (McGahan, 2015: np).

If we take a moment to pause and think about it, the idea of "objectifying yourself" is a difficult one. Is it, in fact, possible to objectify yourself? As the opposite of subjects, objects do not have agency or the ability to control how they are seen by people – or, in fact, how they are treated by them. Surely the very fact of actively presenting oneself and offering oneself to be seen in a certain way must mean, from a logical standpoint, that you are not an object? Kim Kardashian is very rich, and influential through her public visibility. She runs several companies and has a great deal of control over her own life and those of other people. Is that what being an

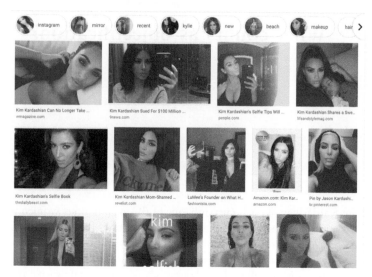

Figure 1.1 Google image search for "Kim Kardashian selfie", March 2020

object means? The fact that Kardashian's celebrity career can be said to result from her objectifying herself suggests how complicated this broadly used notion is, as well as how important it is to understand what it means, how it is used and where its different uses stem from. For what does objectification actually mean?

The concept of objectification has passed out of the realm of academic discussion and feminist politics, and into popular public debate. It is more than a common word used to voice concerns about gender oppression in twenty-first century societies, particularly in connection to the ways that women are represented, and represent themselves, across media. The term bundles together issues about appearance, beauty, bodies, sex and social power. Objectification is one of the most frequently used terms in both academic and media debates on the gendered politics of contemporary culture, and ubiquitous as such. Critiques of objectification range from debates on gendered harassment and discrimination to ones focusing on the sexualization of culture and the pressing presence of gendered body norms within media. Objectification is an issue of media representation and everyday experiences alike, and it cuts through feminist inquiry on an international scale as shorthand for sexist practices of representation and gender-based inequalities. The concept has been used to underpin a number of activist initiatives, from the "we are not things" posters held by #MeToo campaigners to the "National Center on Sexual Exploitation" – a conservative US group – whose complaints about the covers of the *Cosmopolitan* magazine objectifying and demeaning women got the Walmart chain to remove it from checkout counters in 2018. Despite these abundant uses of the term, there is nevertheless surprisingly little consensus as to what qualifies as, or what is meant by, objectification; or how it connects to, and differs from other critical concepts such as sexism or sexualization used for tackling similar concerns. This obscurity is partly due to how the concept is most recurrently used in the context of sexual representation, and as synonymous with the sexual objectification of women.

Setting out to untangle all this, our book uncovers the applications of objectification in feminist scholarship and activism, from 1970s theories of film spectatorship and gendered ways of seeing to anti-pornography discourses and to critiques of body and beauty norms, as carried out under the rubric of sexualization. We are a group of male and female researchers trained in film studies, cultural studies and media studies, queer and straight, working in Australia, Finland and the United Kingdom. We are all strongly committed to feminist approaches to understanding the media and we want to think through the opportunities and the risks that are involved in making critiques of objectification a central part of our attempts to challenge sexist ideologies that devalue and disempower women. We ask, what is at stake in debates connected to objectification, what the possibilities and limitations of the notion are and what other analytical routes are on offer for understanding gender, sexuality and the media. In doing so, we make an argument for the continuing necessity of critiquing *sexism*, namely discrimination or bias based on someone's perceived gender, while simultaneously insisting on the importance of sexual agency and the value of sexual representation – not least to those in disenfranchised social positions. In other words, we argue for distinguishing between critiques of sex in the media and those addressing sexism as a social practice. This connects to our further argument on the centrality of sexual agency and sexual subjectivity – that of women, men and people of other genders – as it connects to practices of representation, self-fashioning and relating to other people: it is our concern that this is something that broad critiques of objectification fail to accommodate.

Mapping objectification

We start by considering the ways in which objectification has been discussed in academic writing. Across its different applications in film and media studies, gender studies, sociology, law, and beyond, objectification means treating and dehumanizing a person as a thing, instrument or object. However, this shared starting point masks a range of complex differences in the way that the term has been employed in diverse contexts, from conditions of slavery to the glossy imageries of advertising – phenomena that are strikingly distinct, involve incompatible relations and dynamics of power and yield drastically different social effects. In her analysis of the understanding of objectification within feminist inquiry, philosopher Martha Nussbaum (1995: 256–7) defines it as "a question of treating one thing as another. One is treating *as an object* what is really not an object, what is in fact, a human being". Nussbaum (1995: 251) argues that objectification remains a slippery concept that can be interpreted in at least seven different ways, "none of which implies any of the others":

1   *Instrumentality*: The objectifier treats the object as a tool of their other purposes.
2   *Denial of autonomy*: The objectifier treats the object as lacking in autonomy and self-determination.
3   *Inertness*: The objectifier treats the object as lacking in agency, and perhaps also in activity.
4   *Fungibility:* The objectifier treats the object as interchangeable (a) with other objects of the same type, and/or (b) with objects of other types.
5   *Violability:* The objectifier treats the object as lacking in boundary-integrity, as something that it is permissible to break up, smash, break into.
6   *Ownership:* The objectifier treats the object as something that is owned by another, can be bought or sold, etc.

7   *Denial of subjectivity:* The objectifier treats the object as
    something whose experience and feelings (if any) need not be
    taken into account (Nussbaum, 1995: 257).

As Nussbaum points out, just because something is an object does
not mean it is seen as worthless or disposable. Some objects – such as
paper coffee cups – are, but others – such as art and antiques – definitely are not. So even from the start it is not clear exactly what
"objecthood" means. On the one hand, Nussbaum identifies all seven
forms of objectification as morally objectionable in blurring and violating the boundaries of objects and human subjects. On the other
hand, none of this is absolute, given the ambiguities involved: a child,
for example, is not granted full individual autonomy, but this is not
necessarily morally problematic, given children's cognitive and affective
limitations of understanding and independently acting out in the world.
We might momentarily instrumentalize an intimate partner, relying on
them to provide something for us. They may never even know that this
has happened, so that it has no impact on their lives. Alternatively, they
may not mind doing us a favour. They may be pleased to be of help, or
they may like us to eye them as desirable sexual objects.
    Importantly – objectification is not automatically about gender,
even though debates on objectification do almost exclusively cluster
on issues having to do with the representation of women. Both
men and women can be objectified and sexualized, across all of the
domains noted above. For example, it makes sense to say that
people of all genders are objectified in capitalist, neo-liberal
societies, even though they are not similarly objectified in different,
differently sexist and patriarchal cultures. In referring to the process of rendering people into things, the notion of objectification is
akin to Georg Lukács's concern with *reification* as a process where
people become thing-like in their behaviours and functions while
man-made objects gain certain liveness within commodity fetish-
ism (see Pitkin, 1987). For Lukács, building on Karl Marx, reification was a product of capitalism and hence entailed a broad
logic of instrumentality and alienation that did not follow the
divides of gender. It is therefore possible to critique the logics of
neoliberalism as a dominant economical and ideological social
framework within which the value of individuals is seen as
dependent on their individual productivity – or, as in the case of

Kim Kardashian, on their sheer visibility. As individuals compete on free markets, they come to understand and to craft themselves into commodities in order to find employment as well as to be valued in their other social relations and attachments. In this framework, neoliberalism is seen as that which makes people make themselves into objects while also commodifying intimate relations as exchanges of human goods and services. Kardashian's self-branding exercises, both individually and together with her similarly famous partner, the rapper Kanye West, are symbolic of success within such markets of neoliberalism.

We can even argue that the very act of representing somebody, in any way – photographing them, say, or recording their voice or shooting their movements on video – also objectifies them in the sense of rendering a person subject of consumption through visual or auditory means. Images of their bodies can be reproduced, contemplated, edited or watched in slow motion; their voice can be replayed, or broken down into sounds to be recomposed at will; their representations can be used for promotional or advertising purposes. This does not mean that the bodies represented are automatically or causally rendered as objects of sexual availability, or that all gendered practices of representation involve the making of sexual objects. Things are more complex.

Gendered objects

We are interested in why sexuality – and heterosexuality in particular – has remained so key to debates on objectification to the point of this being the primary framework within which the term is deployed. Any kind of a person, or animal, can be objectified in the sense of being stripped of autonomy and volition, and being treated as an instrument for the gain of others. The ownership of people as slaves in the United States relied on the objectification of Africans and African-Americans as property rather than people, and as instruments whose lives could be terminated at their owners' will. Such dehumanization is an ultimate reminder of what objectification can mean in terms of denying autonomy and agency to human beings. In this book, we are primarily concerned about objectification as it is used in feminist critique, this being the primary, predominant framework within which the term continues to be deployed.

Ann Cahill argues traces feminist conceptualizations of objectification back to the work of Simone de Beauvoir in the 1940s, who saw the identification of women with the passive materiality of their bodies – their apparent *thingness* – as a primary tactic of gender-based othering. Sexuality, she points out, has since been understood as being key to the formation of women as objects:

> Much of feminist theory has been committed to the claim that the sexual objectification of women is harmful, degrading, and oppressive. To be viewed as a sex object is to be regarded as less than a full human person, to be debased and reduced to mere flesh. The male gaze – which is male primarily in its effect, not necessarily in its origin, in that women can also adopt it – defines and constrains women, assesses their beauty, and in doing so dehumanizes them.
>
> (Cahill, 2011: 84)

What is mainly meant with objectification in feminist critiques is the reduction of women to their physical attributes and heterosexual attractiveness in ways that mitigate their individuality and agency. This is a very real kind of objectification, yet one that hardly compares with the conditions and practices of slavery. Despite the dramatic disparity between these two examples, both connections and equations between the two were drawn in 1970s and 1980s radical feminist writings critiquing women's position within patriarchy and using pornography as key example of the systematic oppression and the enslavement of women. Nussbaum (1995: 249) associates the overall popularity and resonance of the notion of objectification in discussions of gender relations with the work of Andrea Dworkin and Catharine A. MacKinnon built on a broader conceptualization of heterosexuality as entailing the sexual objectification, commodification, and the consequent dehumanization of women by men. This meant understanding pornography as a means of silencing women by making them into things, objects and commodities (Langton, 2009: 10): MacKinnon (1996: 33–7) saw pornographic representations of non-consent as comparable to images of lynchings and genocide as violent expressions of hate. A binary gender divide premised on heterosexual power dynamics cuts through much of this feminist work. As we show in Chapter 3, within this "body politics", sexuality becomes the terrain of power and domination while objectification becomes a process of world-building that "creates reality and types of beings" (Cahill, 2011: 4).

Feminist critiques of objectification have not then been simply concerned with gender stereotypes, or the ways in which men and women are expected to perform different roles in patriarchal societies. Rather, they have attempted to show the processes by which women are cast as lesser to and as subservient to men, as well as how the facts of being represented – depicted, acknowledged and spoken for – are distributed differently for men and for women, giving further rise to gender asymmetry. Much of this has to do with the dynamics of heterosexuality and cultural representations thereof.

As Nussbaum's work shows us, there is however no necessary link between objectification and sexual representation. Research across academic disciplines has addressed a number of contexts in which people are treated as objects in ways that do not involve being sexualized – as in the case of trafficked farm labour, for example. Conversely, people can be and perform sexinesss and contribute to sexual representations without losing their agency – or, at least, we argue this to be the case. Sexism, we further argue, is a different concern from both sexual depiction and sexiness, despite the ease with which these notions are routinely conflated. Sexism is an operation of power that crafts out, and supports unequal social relations by allocating bodies coded as feminine – independent of whether these bodies are cis- or transgender, considered genetically or anatomically female or not – with particular forms of agency, vulnerability and assumed sexual availability. People can be represented as sexually attractive or as engaged in sexual activities, and they can represent themselves as sexually attractive and as engaged in sexual activities without becoming someone else's tools lacking in agency, becoming interchangeable, or being owned. Such depictions are not reducible to any single set of meanings, nor are they simply similar to one another.

Yet the fact remains that different groups of people are assigned different kinds of roles in practices of representation, these roles building on, possibly further fuelling or challenging social hierarchies and relations of power, as drawn along the axes of gender, race, class, sexuality, ability, size, and a plethora of other differences. Different people then fail to be similarly treated: some are seen as being more important and valuable than others, and such differences need to be accounted. The value and importance allocated to people within a society then reverberates with how these people are depicted in the media and how their voices become heard within it. This is key to the politics of cultural representation as it intersects with social power, a concern and a research tradition discussed further in Chapter 2.

Collapsing sex and sexism

As we argue in this book, much contemporary feminist debate collapses together the concepts of sexism and objectification as though these terms were synonyms. The notion of objectification holds perennial appeal as shorthand for gender-based inequalities. There is often seeming immediacy, or acuteness, to critiques of objectification as a means of intervening in public debate: the notion speaks to transformations that we can see happening in the public sphere. This book, again, suggests that one pauses before launching into diagnoses of objectification, and considers instead what the point of the intended analysis and critique is and what one in fact wants to describe with the concept. Is one critiquing the operations of sexism, or acts of sex displayed in the media? Is the issue one of nudity, of commodification and consumer culture or gender-based violence – or all of the above? In particular, this book argues against the equation of sexual representation with sexism.

Western cultures are increasingly sexually permissive, even progressive. Churches have less control over sexual expression than was the case in the past. Moralistic demands that women cover up their bodies are no longer as powerful as was the case in the past. In this context sexual content is increasingly visible, public and diverse. The landscape of mediated sex has drastically expanded and shifted from print, television and film to social media platforms and other networked exchanges hosting commercially produced content, DIY efforts and myriad combinations thereof – from queer tube celebrities to sex education resources and nude selfies. Pornography, a perennial concern in debates on objectification, is available in broader and more diverse supply than ever, further accelerating concerns about the current cultural moment, its impacts on contemporary sexual mores and those to follow (see Attwood, 2017). The ways in which sex and sexuality are discussed and represented are more diverse than ever to date, encompassing not only lesbian and gay perspectives but equally those of asexual, transgender, nonbinary and gender nonconforming people.

Meanwhile, feminist critiques of objectification have responded to such changes primarily by focusing on the commercial uses of female bodies in the media. In their analysis of advertisements that sexually objectify women, Amanda Zimmerman and John Dahlberg (2008), for example, motivate their study through the increased presence of sexual media content:

> For women born in the early 1980s, sex in the media has been a constant companion. Sex is everywhere, on prime-time television programs, movies, and music videos. It is rare to view an hour of television and not see a suggestively dressed or undressed female, whether in a program or a commercial. Sexual imagery appears in magazine articles and advertisements. A recent issue of *Cosmopolitan* might contain hundreds of half-naked women, stories of sexual mishaps, and even instructions for the ancient art of Kama Sutra.
>
> (Zimmerman and Dahlberg, 2008: 71)

This argument is not an isolated one as similar concerns over the increased sexualization and pornification of culture have been vocally posed since the early 2000s. Pamela Paul's book *Pornified: How Pornography is Transforming Our Lives, Our Relationships and Our Families* (Paul, 2005) and Ariel Levy's *Female Chauvinist Pigs: Women and the Rise of Raunch Culture* (Levy, 2005) launched the language of pornification into mainstream public debate and tied concerns about objectification to the notion of sexual liberation and the gendered fallacies it entails. Looking more carefully at Zimmerman and Dahlberg's account of sexual objectification, they conflate sexual content with female nudity as though they are automatically the same thing, without paying attention to contextual differences between, say, images or sex tips in *Cosmopolitan* magazine, the *Kamasutra* as an ancient erotic Hindu text, sexy poses taken in music videos and sex scenes featured in films non-pornographic enough to be shown on prime-time television. The authors equate sexism with portrayals focusing on women's bodies – all kinds of bodies – in ways that leave little room to think about sexism apart from sexual depiction or objectification (Zimmerman and Dahlberg, 2008: 72, 74).

We disagree with this position. We note that despite the accumulation of diagnoses, according to which contemporary culture is increasingly preoccupied with the visual objectification of women, there is actually less sexism in the media now than there was in previous decades. In other words, while there may be more *sexual* depiction than ever, *sexist* representations have grown less socially acceptable, and it is productive to ply these two concepts apart.

Take – an obvious and egregious media historical example – the highly popular British television comedy series, *The Benny Hill Show* (1955–1989) (see Figure 1.2). At least since the 1970s, each episode of this worldwide success ended in a scene of a chase where the main character was chased by people, chased some people himself, or both. As much of the show's comedy was based on instances of heterosexual titillation and female lack of dress, these people were notably often semi-naked women, sometimes in their underwear or strategically clutching a garment to cover their nudity. While the amusement of this recurrent scene might not seem obvious to the contemporary viewer, it

Figure 1.2 In a typical *Benny Hill* sketch, a nurse in an old folks' home plays strip poker with an old man. When she gets down to her bra and panties, the excitement of seeing of her cleavage kills the old man she's playing with

carried well into the series' demise. In another British example, since the 1970s, tabloid newspaper *The Sun* was renowned for its Page 3 Girls – young women who smiled invitingly while baring their breasts in the nation's favourite "newspaper" – the feature gradually disappeared in the course of the 2010s. In 1983 – the heyday of the "Page 3 Stunner" – *The Sun* introduced a counter counting down the days until Samantha Fox (its most famous model) turned sixteen years old and the paper could legally publish topless images of her. Such examples show that previous decades were not spaces of innocent purity with regards to their representations of women.

Further, even when previous decades were less overtly sexual in their representation of women, they were massively more sexist. It is in fact noteworthy that, in thinking of examples of sexist representation, it is the media of yesteryear that first comes to mind. Take the case of a single genre – police shows. The genre emerged in its modern form in the radio show *Dragnet* (1949–1957) and its television version (1951–1959, 1967–1970). Over the course of its television life, *Dragnet* had six lead characters – all male. Of course, women *appeared* – in roles as secretaries, wives and mothers, and particularly as victims of crime. Women were not police: in a sexist culture, entertainment reflected that sexism. The cop show flourished in succeeding decades, with forty-two new programmes debuting in America in the 1970s (Butler, 2004: 1870). It wasn't until *Police Woman* (1974) that a female police officer headlined a TV show. The lead character, Sergeant "Pepper" Anderson (Angie Dickinson) worked in an undercover unit, and in the course of the show went undercover as a model, an airline stewardess, a sex worker (or, as used in the show, "prostitute"), and a go-go dancer among other roles. It is interesting that the next major crime show with female leads, *Charlie's Angels* (1976–1981), also featured the heroines regularly going undercover as models, night club dancers, roller-skating waitresses, and sex workers (or, as used in the show, "streetwalkers") (see Figure 1.3). As *Charlie's Angels* ended, *Cagney and Lacey* became, in 1982, the first cop show to feature female cops who were not regularly going undercover, but were just getting on with being cops – and even here the role of Cagney was recast after the first season because, as a CBS executive put it in an interview with *TV Guide*: "The American public doesn't respond to the bra burners, the fighters, the women who insist on calling manhole covers peoplehole covers ... We perceived them [actors Tyne Daly and Meg Foster] as dykes" (Butler, 2004: 1780).

Figure 1.3 A female TV detective in 1977: Cheryl Ladd in *Charlie's Angels* episode "Pretty Angels All in a Row"

In our current television ecology dozens of crime shows have female leads – *The Bridge, Line of Duty, The Killing, No Offence, Broadchurch, The Fall, Elementary, The Closer, Cold Case, Bones, Without A Trace, Law and Order: SVU,* and so on. These characters are not required to go undercover as sex workers, they get the job done and are not simply recast because producers fear audiences perceive some of them as dykes. In this context it is sobering to remember how far we have come in terms of entertainment. For twenty-five years women watching television did not see a single female lead in a cop show. After that, when they did see women, they were going undercover in traditionally feminine occupations (in neither *Police Woman* nor *Charlie's Angels* did a woman go undercover as a surgeon or a politician, for example). It took thirty years for female viewers to see a female cop leading a show who was not performing stereotyped feminine roles as part of her duties. That is a massively sexist entertainment culture.

We can trace similar changes in other genres, as the roles played by women have expanded and become more authoritative and less reliant on being wives, mothers and secretaries. Media representations of women in the twenty-first century are less sexist than fifty years ago, and this correlates with the increased presence of women in positions of political, corporate, cultural and financial leadership. This is not to say that the current world of entertainment is perfect – that is far from the case. Representations of able-bodied young bodies displayed for the visual gratification of viewers remain standard and ubiquitous. But in the media now these bodies are not exclusively female or feminine, nor are they merely catering to the visual pleasures of male heterosexual audiences.

In short, the current range of sexual representation in Western cultures is not correlated with increasing sexism in those cultures. In terms of gender representation and attitudes towards women, we believe that anybody who has any familiarity with cultural history would agree that society and, by extension, the media is less sexist now than was the case in previous decades. Even if, in cop shows, women were not being shown topless as such, they could only be secretaries, aspiring at most to make cups of tea for the men who actually went out and did the work (when *Charlie's Angel* Sabrina left the show at the start of season five it was because she was going to get married and start a family; there was no suggestion that a woman could get married, start a family, and continue solving crimes). There are many forms of sexism that remain unconnected to the sexualization of female bodies – and we should avoid romanticizing the past, or insisting that the world was absolutely less sexist until the broad availability of online pornography, for example.

Viewing historical examples of such sexist representation in contemporary media studies classrooms usually results in confusion, bemusement and dismay. They simply come across as incompatible with contemporary conventions of representation, and bizarre in the gendered and sexual dynamics that they depict. While relatively recent historically, they speak of an alien cultural context where the lines of acceptability in terms of representation, humour, gendered agency and heterosexual titillation were differently drawn. They further speak of contexts where explicit sexism was not only acceptable it was taken for granted, and even expected in popular media representation, and their existence certainly challenges arguments that identify sexually suggestive poses or innuendos as a development specific to the recent emergence of "porn culture" (e.g. Sarracino and Scott, 2008: x). As there is no evidence of media culture having grown ever more sexist with the abundant supply of sexual content, this book argues that it is imperative to distinguish between sex and sexism, sexual representation and sexist representation, if we are to understand the different meanings, roles and values of the depictions in question.

Things to come

This book explores the risks of conflating sexuality and sexism, objectification and sexism, or objectification and sexual depiction. The following chapters take you through the history of debates about objectification and gendered representation from the 1970s to the current day, analysing the stakes involved in and for feminist theory and activism, and sets out to find alternative ways of thinking about sexism, representation and sexual agency. All this necessitates going back to what are by now classics texts on the politics of vision and object-making before moving onto analyses of contemporary media culture.

Chapter 2 starts our argument by tracing the importance of John Berger's (1972) book, *Ways of Seeing*, and Laura Mulvey's (1975) classic essay, "Visual Pleasure and Narrative Cinema", for their theorizations of the dynamics of gendered forms of representation, looking and spectatorship. Despite being published in the 1970s, both bodies of work, and that of Mulvey's in particular, remain widely cited and are still used to provide a framework for understanding the gender dynamics of vision today, foregrounding gendered social power and control in practices of seeing and being seen. Considering the multiple legacies and uses of Mulvey's essay, the chapter also asks how it has been challenged and how it connects to later studies investigating the role of representation in the construction of gender roles and the ways that men and women are differently valued. This contextual chapter then presents key questions in studies of looking, gender and power.

Chapter 3 asks why, out of all the different aspects of objectification that we might consider, sexuality has been, and remains, so central to feminist debates on this topic. We explain this by looking at the work of radical feminist writers of the 1970s and 1980s, exploring how this work drew attention to the ideologies of gender in society and which created a series of binaries whereby male/female is mapped onto a series of other values – active/passive, strong/weak, subject/object. This framework continues to hold power in ways of thinking about and acting against gender oppression, yet the binary model poses severe limitations to how gender can be thought of and, consequently, in how objects of critique are identified and approached. We ask how this model has fed into ways of understanding, valuing and denouncing sexual practices, as well as how it relates to changing social structures, particularly the challenge of intersectional thinking about power and transgender identity.

In Chapter 4, having established why representations of sex have become the key way of thinking about objectification and the symbolic role that pornography has occupied in these debates, we move to thinking about sexual subjectivity in connection with sex work. For those feminist activists and researchers seeing pornography as the most powerful form of objectification, the agency of women producing it has come across as limited, or even illusory. Resisting a binary between sexual depiction as objectification and sexual subjectivity, we address the pornographic work of Jiz Lee, arguing that it undermines any conflation of sexual performance with a position of powerlessness. In contrast, such claims can be seen as dependent on, and as reinvigorating, sexist tropes of appropriate femininities. In doing so, the chapter teases out complexities and nuances connected to the work of commercial sex and the sexual agency enacted within it.

In Chapter 5, we ask how objectification can be measured in academic research and how the concept intersects with concerns over sexualization in the field of social psychology in particular – how, in fact, objectification as a concern about body image shifted to, and merged with, concerns over sexualization. In doing so, we shift our focus to methodological choices and challenges involved in identifying objectification in pornographic representations, and beyond. The chapter shows the debt of objectification theories to models of media effects, asking how perceptions of negative impact build on, and tap into, norms concerning what is seen as healthy or normal sexuality, as the discussion extends from investigations of pornography as a highly contested terrain of cultural production and consumption to sexually suggestive forms of popular media.

Having explored how the wide variety of debates about sexism and representation have often been reduced down to concern about pornography, in Chapter 6, we show how concern has, once more, extended to representations of women in a range of popular media genres. The concepts of "pornification" and "sexualization" have been used to diagnose broad cultural transformations within which the objectification of women occurs. Our interests lie in how a sexualization debate has emerged with an established rhetoric, range of figures, narratives and particular concerns, and how it maps to the notion of objectification. By addressing academic studies and government reports alike, we inquire after the gendered and sexual norms that they communicate while also focusing on the difficulties of evaluating or defining sexual agency. Concluding with the example of pop star Ariana Grande's uses of "sexiness" in her performance style, we argue for complicating over-arching interpretations of what such representations may mean or achieve.

In Chapter 7, we explore alternative ways of approaching and addressing gendered modes of seeing and being seen, in tandem with looking for alternative terminology to that of the male gaze in the context of contemporary popular media culture. Taking cue from intersectional critique, the chapter examines music videos by black female artists, showing how their work complicates and disturbs the model of the male gaze (as introduced in Chapter 2), pushing for more diverse and contextual conceptualizations of sexual representation instead. By addressing the reality TV show, *RuPaul's Drag Race* and the 2015 independent film on black transgender sex workers, *Tangerine*, we further point out the shortcomings of theories of objectification and sexualization in being too totalizing and bound up with considerations of binary gender difference, and hence lacking in crucial contextual nuance of the kind necessary for exploring the intersections of identity categories such as race, sexuality or class with that of gender.

Lastly, as a means of drawing these strands of discussion together, Chapter 8 proposes ways forward for research that are not limited to binary divisions between objects and subjects in future considerations of gender, media, sexuality and agency. By focusing on debates and research on selfie culture, we argue for seeing humans simultaneously as subjects and objects, as well as for shifting the emphasis of feminist critique to sexism over sexual representation. All in all, this book argues for an understanding of subjectivity and objecthood as coexistent, rather than as mutually exclusive. As material, embodied beings, we are always already objects, as well as subjects acting out in the world and establishing connections with other bodies within it – a point elaborated in the concluding chapter in particular. There is a plethora of ways to represent, and self-represent such bodies, for one's own pleasure as well as for the pleasure of others. Within these, it is possible to be represented as an object of visual pleasure as a flirtatious invitation, as an offer of services, or as a way of perceiving oneself from a distance: none of this implies or necessitates an annulment of agency or subjectivity. Furthermore, none of these practices need be confined in a heteronormative framework premised on binary gender.

As feminist authors, we have spent our careers examining the ways in which gender identities, relations and oppression are supported and made meaningful in media practices. From this perspective we are concerned that the ways in which the concept of "objectification" gets used in both public debates and academic inquiry fails to do the crucial work in prying apart sexism from sexual representation and, consequently, fails in examining the crucial issues concerning social power that are at play. We want to offer what we see as some more useful ways to think about and challenge sexism in popular media and in our societies. We hope that this book will be useful in helping you think about these issues, too.

2 Male gaze and the politics of representation

Many different social institutions and processes are understood to contribute to gender inequality, sexism and patriarchal ideology, yet media representations of women remain a particular focus for protests against objectification. In this chapter, we look at the emergence of feminist concerns about representation, and in particular the relationship of representation to the act and the dynamics of looking in the 1970s that paved way for later debates on objectification while also giving rise to persistent analytical stances in academic studies of gender, vision and spectatorship. As we discuss, ways of seeing and being seen have been theorized in terms of a gendered dichotomy whereby looking is understood to be active and masculine, while being looked at has been presented as passive and feminine. Feminist studies of film have been influential in the evolution of this idea, particularly in relation to ideas of "the male gaze" and spectatorship. This chapter traces the evolution of these ideas, the stakes involved in debates on gendered vision, and their expansion by a range of cultural critics and theorists.

Looking and being looked at

The concept of "the male gaze", as introduced by feminist film theorist Laura Mulvey, has become the concept that is most commonly applied in thinking about why representation matters to understanding both patriarchy and sexism. Despite being coined through analysis of classical Hollywood cinema (of the 1930s through the 1950s), the male gaze has grown into shorthand for gendered politics of vision in a range of media and practices of everyday life, spanning several decades.

The prehistory of the notion of "the male gaze" and its popularization can however be dated to 1972 and *Ways of Seeing*, a television series about the history of art created and presented by English art critic John Berger. At the start of the second episode, Berger informs us that "Men dream of women, women dream of themselves being dreamt of. Men look at women. Women watch themselves being looked at" and that "Women constantly meet glances, which act like mirrors, reminding them how they look or how they should look. Behind every glance is a judgement. Sometimes the glance they meet is their own reflected from a real mirror." In the book of the same name that has since assumed a foundational status in the study of visual culture, Berger summarizes his thesis yet more emphatically: "*men act* and *women appear* ... the surveyor of woman in herself is male: the surveyed female. Thus she turns herself into an object – and most particularly an object of vision: a sight" (Berger, 1972: 47).

In both book and TV series, Berger implicitly draws together a range of theoretical positions and approaches including ideas derived from the Frankfurt school (critiquing the culture industry since the 1930s), political economy, feminism and psychoanalysis, in order to gender the act of looking. He argues that women regard themselves as objects and subject to the scrutiny of being "looked at" and lastly, perhaps most radically, that women can only see themselves through the eyes of men. Berger's argument is grounded in analysis of the gendered nature of subject/object relations to be found in many famous paintings from Western fine art traditions. For example, he compares the expression of Ingres' *La Grande Odalisque* (1814) to a pin-up example from a "girlie" magazine, arguing that both expressions are dream-like and passive. In 1972, this comparison would have seemed challenging but Berger's substantive point is that the rhetoric of sexuality that is written into commercial imagery has its precedent in examples of elite culture. So he suggests that:

> Is not the [woman's] expression remarkably similar in each case? It is the expression of a woman responding with calculated charm to the man whom she imagines looking at her – although she doesn't know him. She is offering up her femininity as the surveyed.
>
> (Berger, 1972: 56)

Berger's work has been massively influential. The fact that these ideas now seem commonplace is testament to how much they have become part of our everyday thinking about gender and representation. At the time of his writing, feminist art history was only becoming visible as a critical field of investigation through the work of authors such as Linda Nochlin. The mainstream of art criticism had not interrogated the differences in representation between men and women – it was simply the case that men would be depicted as active, with weapons and horses, whereas women would be in repose, scantily clad and languid. Berger contributed to a language for challenging the naturalness of such depictions and for interrogating why things were the way they were, influencing both feminist art historical research and more mainstream forms of cultural critique.

The male gaze

A year after Berger's TV series was aired, feminist filmmaker and film theorist Laura Mulvey wrote the essay "Visual Pleasure and Narrative Cinema" that was eventually published in *Screen* in 1975. The author and the essay are best known for coining the term the "male gaze", a concept which has migrated from describing specific conditions of film representation and spectatorship to become part of a popular debate around the representation of women's bodies across media. Mulvey's work went further than Berger by explicitly politicizing the gendered relations of looking through critical analysis of the pleasures of mainstream, narrative cinema and their fantasy of man as active, desiring subject and woman as passively desired. From the outset of the essay, Mulvey declares her radical political intentions, claiming to want to put her insights to "political use" and furthermore to do that in order to "destroy pleasure" gained from Hollywood cinema. Such destruction would, she hoped, result in the development of a new language of desire.

In order to effect this, Mulvey drew on the language and concepts of psychoanalysis. Psychoanalysis, originally developed as therapeutic intervention for mental disorders in Sigmund Freud's work, offered ways of conceiving the workings of the "unconscious" – that part of the human mind that is unknowable, even to ourselves. During the 1970s, psychoanalytical theory became a popular, widely influential approach in film studies for researchers who were interested in the relationship between films, identity and pleasure.

In bringing psychoanalysis to bear on explaining the politics of spectatorial relations, Mulvey drew firstly on Freud's *Three Essays on Sexuality* to establish her theoretical framework. In particular, Mulvey addressed his writing about the pleasure in looking – scopophilia – as a drive that takes "other people as objects, subjecting them to a controlling and curious gaze" (Mulvey, 1975: 8). Mulvey argues that Hollywood cinema is the perfect example of scopophilia, offering images of women for the visual pleasure of men, and thus reinforcing an inequal gender binary by "cod[ing] the erotic into the language of the dominant patriarchal order" (ibid). All this involves voyeurism, sexual pleasure taken in watching others when they are unaware of being seen – a relationship laced with libidinous overtones inasmuch as with an unbalance of power.

Secondly, Mulvey refers to the work of Jacques Lacan and his 1949 theory of "the mirror stage" which argued that the point at which a child encounters and recognizes its reflection in a mirror is a fundamental moment for ego formation and also a point at which both recognition and misrecognition takes place. The child sees an image of itself and imagines the image to be a superior and more complete version of itself. That is to say, Lacan believed that before recognizing its own image in a mirror, the child is not a coherent human subject, but a bundle of disparate impulses, feelings and desires, there being no preceding sense of "I".

At this point we should make the methodological note that psychoanalysis is a profoundly anti-empirical form of knowledge in the sense that it does not seek "proof" for its theories. In terms of theory-formation, it is not elementary whether there is evidence that children do not have a sense of themselves as coherent subjects until they recognize themselves in a mirror, or after. Indeed, it may be that this is only a metaphor. Adding to the challenge, nonconscious processes, by definition, can never be accessed by the conscious mind. Psychoanalysis seeks to understand how subjects are formed. Psychoanalytical film theory examines the issue through audiovisual analysis of chosen cinematic examples: it does not, for example, expand into empirical inquiry into practices of filmmaking or spectatorship. Viewers, as discussed in this framework, are textual positions implicated by films (as "text"), not actual viewers as such. As a methodological approach, psychoanalysis is both highly specific and specifically limited.

Mulvey argues that Lacan's idea of the "mirror stage" is important for feminism because "it is an image that constitutes the matrix of the imaginary, of recognition/misrecognition and identification, and hence of the first articulation of the 'I', of subjectivity" (Mulvey, 1975: 9). That is to say, human beings, who as babies are messy and contradictory bundles of impulses and feelings, reach a stage where they become aware of the culture around them, that they begin to understand the cultural requirement for a single and coherent sense of "I" – a subject position – and that there are particular requirements as to what kind of subject the child ought to become. Mulvey argues that cinema spectatorship is similar to this "mirror stage": "The long love affair/despair between image and self-image ... has found such intensity of expression in film and such joyous recognition in the cinema audience ... quite apart from the extraneous similarities between screen and mirror" (Mulvey, 1975: 10).

With her political intentions made explicit and an engagement with extremely dense theory acknowledged, in the section of the essay entitled, "Woman as Image, Man as Bearer of the Look" Mulvey presents the heart of her argument built around a conceptual scaffolding synthesizing psychoanalysis with Marxist theory:

> In a world ordered by sexual imbalance, pleasure in looking has been split between active/male and passive/female. The determining male gaze projects its fantasy onto the female figure, which is styled accordingly. In their traditional exhibitionist role women are simultaneously looked at and displayed, with their appearance coded for strong visual and erotic impact so that they can be said to connote *to-be looked-at-ness*. ... The presence of woman is an indispensable element of spectacle in normal narrative film, yet her visual presence tends to work against the development of a story-line, to freeze the flow of action in moments of erotic contemplation.
>
> (Mulvey, 1975: 11, emphasis in the original)

Mulvey's analysis draws on a broad range of examples of Hollywood cinema including Sternberg's *Morocco* (1930), *To Have and Have Not* (Howard Hawks, 1944) and *Vertigo* (Alfred Hitchcock, 1958), as well as Marilyn Monroe's performance in *The River of no Return*

(Preminger, Negulesco, 1954). Monroe's presentation as sexual spectacle is remarkably consistent across all of her screen appearances: for instance, when Monroe is introduced in *Some Like it Hot* (Billy Wilder, 1959) she epitomizes Mulvey's notion of "looked-at-ness" (see Figure 2.1). Joe and Jerry (Tony Curtis and Jack Lemmon), on the run from the mafia and disguised as female musicians, are halted midway through their conversation when Sugar Cane (Monroe) walks along the platform to board the train. Not only does she literally stop their conversation but also the narrative of the film in its tracks. In a cloche hat with extravagant feather, fur trimmed cinched coat and carrying a ukulele, Monroe is filmed in mid-shot and soft-focus which then cuts to a reaction shot of the two male leads, and then a reverse shot of Monroe's legs and behind, eroticizing her heels and stockings and provocative body movement. The spectacle of Monroe in this now famous cinematic fragment both disrupts narrative flow and forces us to see the star through the male gaze as a sexual object in the way that Mulvey describes. Indeed, the mise-en-scène of the film – an eruption of steam from the underside of the train that almost knocks Monroe off her feet – seems to shoo her away in order to restart the narrative flow. In essence, Mulvey argues that patriarchy and the products of its institutions such as classical Hollywood cinema compel us to see the

Figure 2.1 Marilyn Monroe in *Some Like it Hot* (1959)

world through a three-layered male gaze, one encompassing the male eyes of the camera/the director, those of male characters within film and those of its implied viewers. According to Mulvey, in film, the camera looks at women, we see men looking at women and we, as viewers, look at women as fetishized objects.

Responses to 'Visual Pleasure and Narrative Cinema'

Within the academy, Mulvey's essay provoked significant debate which built on and developed the concept of the male gaze – as in Mary Ann Doane's (1980) "Misrecognition and Identity". The concept was critiqued for example in Gaylyn Studlar's essay "Masochism and the Perverse Pleasures of the Cinema", which described Mulvey's model as "deterministic [and] polarized" and as involving "a crucial 'blind spot' in her theory of visual pleasure" (Studlar, 1984: 274). In "Recent Developments in Feminist Criticism" Christine Gledhill (1978) called for understanding and analyses of representations of women within patriarchal culture that move beyond a focus on the analysis of texts alone to consider conditions of production and consumption, opening up the possibility of a "female gaze" (see below). The debate continued not least because, as David Rodowick notes, Mulvey's essay has been read more literally and prescriptively than it was intended (Rodowick, 1991: 4).

Indeed, although the essay's argument is deceptively, perhaps seductively, easy to grasp, its overall logic hinges on specific theoretical, psychoanalytical premises. The essay builds on a firm gender binary structured by the dynamics of male heterosexual desire that is complicated by the castration anxiety that, following Freud, is key to the formation of male subjects. As acute reminder of women's castrated state, the female body in film needs to be objectified and presented as fetishized body parts – legs, lips, breasts – that, as fetishes, function as stand-ins for the lacking penis. Since scopophilia connected to the male gaze is understood as a controlling, even sadistic drive, female viewers are left with the option of masochistic pleasure in the face of their own objectification. There is no room for the active desire of female viewers, no room for identifications that cross the gender binary.

It is also worth noting that Mulvey herself revised (or perhaps clarified) her position, noting that "the male gaze" is not as monolithic as her earlier article had suggested. In "Afterthoughts on 'Visual Pleasure and Narrative Cinema' inspired by King Vidor's

Duel in the Sun (1946)" she writes about both female spectatorship and instances in popular cinema where the protagonist is female. Here she argues that, in classical Hollywood cinema at least, woman always "signifies" sexuality (Mulvey, 1989: 32). In *Death 24x a Second*, Mulvey (2006) further acknowledges that it is not always true that "the gaze" is male and represents male power over women, particularly (she argues) because of technological change and the way it has given viewers the ability to control and therefore make sense of images. Such developments, for Mulvey, unravel the three-fold structure of the male gaze, allowing for more diverse ways of seeing and being seen.

Other academics have challenged the idea of "the male gaze" by thinking about the ways that women look at culture – that is, the possibility of a "female gaze". One tradition of activism seeks to challenge patriarchy by calling for different kinds of representation, as in Clare Johnston's essay "Women's Cinema as Counter Cinema" that preceded Mulvey's:

> In order to counter our objectification in the cinema, our collective fantasies must be released: women's cinema must embody the working through of desire: such an objective demands the use of the entertainment film ... it will be from these insights that a genuinely revolutionary conception of counter-cinema for the women's struggle will come.
>
> (Johnston, 1973: 30)

Scholars sought to theorize female spectatorship and the possibility of a "female gaze", but for many feminist theorists the conditions of patriarchy rendered the female gaze all but impossible without a radical revision of gendered patterns of representation. Doane's essay "Film and the Masquerade: Theorising the Female Spectator" typified this pessimistic conclusion:

> Given the structures of cinematic narrative, the woman who identifies with a female character must adopt a passive or masochistic position, while identification with the active hero necessarily entails an acceptance of what Laura Mulvey refers to as a certain "masculinisation" of spectatorship.
>
> (Doane, 1982: 80)

From this perspective "the male gaze" remains inescapable – the act of looking is always male, and always an expression of power over women – even when it is women doing the looking, whether they are looking at women, or looking at other men. Doane's work was informed by Freud, Christian Metz and Mulvey, but also owes a debt to the then relatively new developments in French feminism and in particular the work of Luce Irigaray and Hélène Cixous. Famously expelled from the École Freudienne in Paris in 1974 for her critique of Freud's writings on femininity, Irigaray argued that patriarchy has denied women ability to express or to represent themselves and that "femininity is a role, an image, a value, imposed upon women by male systems of representation" (Irigaray, 1985: 84). Contrasting the singular, goal driven and phallic male sexuality with the diffuse and multiple nature of female sexuality, Cixous called for an "écriture feminine" – a mode of representation grounded in and speaking of the female body and sexuality – in order to overturn patriarchal ideology.

Counterintuitively perhaps, feminist writers and artists suggested that, according to these theories, it was possible to challenge the patriarchal order through the expression of a feminine sexuality grounded in the same bodies that patriarchy reduces women to. If a woman's appearance really does depend on the masculine gaze, so these writers argued, then that offers the possibility for women to stage-manage that "surveillance", through taking control of that visual economy – expressing their agency by managing the sexual representations that patriarchy demands of them. Photographers such as Diane Arbus and Germaine Krull enthusiastically took to the task of portraying themselves, their bodies and social stereotypes to expose the structures of viewing. Many female artists looked to the insights of psychoanalysis to reshape notions of femininity through explicit performance of the feminine self as a masquerade. A concept outlined in Joan Riviere's 1929 essay, "Womanliness as a Masquerade", explaining that women wear femininity as a mask so that they fit into the social world codified by men – "Womanliness" and its proper performance means safety from men's reprisals (Riviere, 1999). The idea of femininity as a masquerade was taken up by a number of photographers who found its conception of distortion and disguise useful to explore the ways the female-self is always concealed.

Perhaps the most famous of these explorations is by "The Heroine with a Thousand Faces", photographer Cindy Sherman who produced a series of sixty-nine black-and-white photographs featuring herself as characters in fictitious Hollywood movies of the kind Mulvey explored in her original essay. Working in the late 1970s, Sherman attempted to re-create the "fifti-ness" style of filmmaking in order to speak to women who had grown up with those heroines. Using vintage clothing, wigs and make-up she played a range of stereotypical female roles photographed as they sat on their own, lost in their own thoughts or perhaps talking to someone out of shot. Using high contrast and light and shadow, the photographed woman is made to stand out from the background, vulnerable to the world around her. In Sherman's photographs we see the socially prescribed roles of housewife, lover or film star, and we also see that those roles are entirely artificial – the dresses made of lace and the pearls around her neck, the make-up and high heels are just part of the performance. By performing this version of femininity, Sherman set out to reject the stereotype, the objectified woman. By showing woman as mask/costume/performance Sherman intended to subvert the male gaze – these "witty parody of media images of women" (Williamson, 2006: 52) made it impossible to fix the identity of the woman in the picture.

The politics of representation

We have spent some time explaining the psychoanalytic underpinnings of Mulvey's writing and key feminist academic responses to it, but in a sense this is not the most important part of our history connected to objectification. The impact of her writing has been immense – but mainly in how the term "the male gaze" has been taken up to argue that men looking at women entails a form of power; and that for women, to be looked at, is a form of powerlessness. The psychoanalytic work that allowed Mulvey to get to this point has largely fallen away in the later uses of the male gaze. The term has become so commonplace that, for example, Diane Ponterotto's 2016 work on the "canonical female body" in "Resisting the Male Gaze: Feminist Responses to the 'Normatization' of the Female Body in Western Culture" makes no mention of Mulvey's essay, nor makes an attempt to critically engage with this gendered conceptualization of spectatorship: it simply refers to "the male gaze" as an (apparently) straightforward and self-evident concept. "The male gaze" continues to be taught across film and media studies courses as a core concept, and it remains in ample use in gender studies classes. As a phrase, rather than as an analytical concept, it has become part of the much broader popular vocabulary of objectification, used to describe sexist and or sexualized representations of women's bodies.

"The male gaze" has become a key phrase for arguments about objectification, drawing attention to the importance of representation in maintaining sexist attitudes and institutions in society. The concept nevertheless operates in a totalizing way through its premise of binary gender. Here, Mulvey's approach finds resonance with radical feminist approaches to representation. Catharine MacKinnon, for example, has considered words and images as the means of placing people in hierarchies, and as key to "how social stratification is made to seem inevitable and right, how feelings of inferiority and superiority are engendered, and how indifference to violence against those on the bottom is rationalized and normalized" (MacKinnon, 1996: 31). Representation is here seen as a monolithic apparatus generating uniform ideological outcomes.

Similarly, radical feminist writer Susanne Kappeler argues in her 1986 book *The Pornography of Representation* (upon which MacKinnon builds her own discussion of representation) that representation is a process of generating not only objects but also subjects, these two categories being firmly mutually exclusive. Importantly, in systems of representation: "The objectification of women means the simultaneous subjectification of men" (Kappeler, 1986: 49), making the objectification of women a pressing concern for the reproduction of male hegemony. Kappeler argues that the objectification of women is structural, whereas the choice of placing men as objects of vision and desire is precisely that; a choice that does not undermine men's categorical access to subjectivity that has been disallowed for women. For her, images of women and men stem from a fundamental gender unbalance, due to which the objectification of men is logically impossible. Representations, as understood here, are figments of male imagination and, in this sense, violent misrepresentations involving the silencing of women as objects of visual gratification, for culture "is patriarchy's self-image" and "image is made in the image of its maker, after its likeness, and not the other way around" (Kappeler, 1986: 31, 53, 61) and hence does not speak of the needs, fantasies, or desires of women but those of men. Kappeler assumes the mutual exclusivity of subjects and objects; the lack of female subjectivity; the operation of gender as built on a binary; and identifying those dynamics as necessitated by and occasioning male heterosexual desire, sexism, and misogyny.

Alongside such approaches, other theories of representation pay attention to social relations of power without simply saying that the gaze is always male, and always an expression of men's power over women. The work of film theorist Richard Dyer, for example, in his 1993 book *The Matter of Images: Essays on Representation*, has been much less influential in public debates than that of Mulvey or MacKinnon but is important in academic thinking in its more expansive approach to cultural meaning-making. Dyer agrees that representation is linked to social power:

> How a group is represented, presented over again in cultural forms, how an image of a member of a group is taken as representative of that group, how that group is represented in the sense of being spoken for and on behalf of (whether they represent, speak for themselves or not), these all have to do with how members of groups see themselves and others like themselves, how they see their place in society, their right to the rights a society claims to ensure its citizens. Equally re-presentation, representativeness, representing have to do also with how others see members of a group and their place and rights, others who have the power to affect that place and those rights. How we are seen determines in part how we are treated; how we treat others is based on how we see them; such seeing comes from representation.
>
> (Dyer, 1993: 1)

Following Dyer, all representation of social groups is political as a form of world-making, yet all representation is also, by definition, partial in that it involves a part standing for a whole; as in an individual standing in for a social group. Critique is then, from the perspective of the politics of representation, a means of intervening in how women, as a group or category, are seen and treated, as well as to impact the ways in which women see themselves and others as citizens with due rights.

Dyer's definition of representation may not seem all too distant from that offered by MacKinnon or Kappeler. However, there are central differences in their understanding of how social hierarchies and representations operate as they are in their views on the fixity of social hierarchies and the availability of tactics of resistance. While Berger's analysis of ways of seeing, Mulvey's male gaze, and the radical feminist analyses of MacKinnon and Kappeler all operate within and through binary notions of gender – where women are represented, objects and powerless, men the ones doing the representing, subjects and powerful – Dyer draws more on a model of society proposed by philosopher Michel Foucault (1990). For Foucault, power is a key dynamic of social structures, but not monolithic or repressive inasmuch as productive. In different cultures at different times, power operates differently, resulting in different social relations, subject positions, ways of seeing and knowing. Every attempt to exercise power results in acts of resistance – that is, power also produces resistance.

Similarly to feminist critics of the 1970s and 1980s, Dyer understands representation as social activity that does not merely reflect but actively produces social hierarchies between, and the ways of understanding, diverse social groups. His conceptualization is not, however, locked into a heteronormative framework, nor does it presume the mutual exclusivity of being a subject and being an object of representation. This distinction is crucial – a practice which disturbs, and ultimately undoes, many of the premises underlining theories of gendered vision, looking, and power that historically underpin debates on objectification. Arguing that representation is always to a certain extent a process of objectification in that it frames and presents individuals and groups as objects of vision and interpretation does not necessarily mean understanding the framework within which that happens as being unequivocally fuelled by heterosexist desire or as involving male dominance and the lack of female agency. People of different genders, ages, ethnicities and sexual orientations can create and consume representations, positioning themselves as objects of vision and desire.

Machines of representation

Mulvey's analysis of the three-fold male gaze results from a context where it is presumed that male screenwriters wrote scripts for

Hollywood films in studios led by men, directed, shot and edited by men. While women were lucrative target groups for Hollywood cinema – not least in genres such as romance, melodrama and the musical – the overall machinery at play was very much governed by men, just as the examples that Berger picks out from the history of art and 1970s England speak of male-dominated societies allocating distinctly different roles and forms of agency to people according to their perceived gender. The example of the television cop show addressed in the introduction to this book, where female agency was long both contested and confined, further describes a field of cultural production steeped in male-dominance, heteronormativity and sexism. While we continue to complicate this gendered power dynamic in the chapters to follow, it is necessary to elaborate further on the overall context and point of the critiques made, if we are to fully understand the framework within which the notion of objectification has become instrumentalized, and the resonance that it has continued to find in feminist scholarship and activism.

Critiques of the male gaze, in short, emerged in a context where structural inequalities in media production where striking, and they resonated with concerns over the shape and form that contemporary gendered representations were taking. In her 1974 polemic, *From Reverence to Rape: The Treatment of Women in the Movies*, feminist film critic Molly Haskell classified representations of women in popular cinema from silent film to the late 1980s in search of positive and liberating role models among the narrow and stereotypical ones (Haskell, 1974). Paving the way to what became identified as "images of women criticism" (see Moi, 1985), Haskell both critiqued what she saw as fallacious gendered depiction and looked for forms of resistance in genres such as the woman's film allowing space for female experiences and perspectives. This trajectory of investigation later continued in feminist scholarship examining both the ideological frictions within and the pleasures afforded by formulaic genre fiction, and popular culture more broadly, to its female consumers.

While Ellen McCracken (1993: 132), in her reading of women's magazines, identified such pleasures as passive in their utopian, unattainable character, Ien Ang (1985) and Janice Radway (1984) examined soap opera and romance, respectively, as temporal releases and emotional negotiations concerning intimate and domestic gendered relations of power. Other feminist critics, such as Germaine Greer in her bestselling 1970 book, *The Female Eunuch*, searching for explanations for women's refusal to throw off their oppression and to revolt against patriarchal structures of power, identified women's magazines and romance as ideological vehicles of power keeping women in their place. As we discuss in Chapter 3, it was nevertheless the genre of pornography, in its forms catering primarily to heterosexual male consumers, that became solidified as the blueprint for sexist representation supporting patriarchal ideology through the objectification of women.

In order to understand this nexus of feminist critique and its diverse objects, it is necessary to acknowledge the different theoretical frameworks and premises within which individual critics have operated – from Mulvey's combination of psychoanalysis and Marxist theory to Kappeler's radical feminist premise of patriarchy as a systematic practice of female oppression and to Ang's and Radway's interest in ambiguous instances of pleasure as key to the appeal of popular culture. Mulvey operated broadly within the tenets of apparatus theory, according to which cinema is ideological in its pursuit of representing reality – in fact, a machine manufacturing images of reality to accommodate and further ideological goals. This claim is not distant from radical feminist insistence on representation as the crafting of patriarchy's self-image, yet with the difference that the former identifies the apparatus of cinema as a tool of ideology, whereas the latter sees all representation as resulting in the same outcome.

A crucial dividing line between different approaches to gender and popular representation lies in the introduction of cultural studies into academic inquiry in the course of the 1980s. This entailed a shift from interpreting meanings of a cultural text – such as a film or an advert – through the means of textual analysis to considerations of multiple modes of interpretation tied to social categories and identities such as gender, race and class. While for Mulvey, the meanings of a film were construed by the apparatus of Hollywood cinema, cultural studies expanded inquiry into empirical viewers through reception studies and by highlighting the mundane contexts and nuances within which cultural objects are consumed, as in the work of Ang and Radway. Such contextual considerations have not always been key to more popular forms of criticism, images of women criticism included, that have tended to postulate much more straightforward media effects ranging from the harms of negative stereotypes to the empowering potentials of positive representations.

While the film and media industries of today are hardly identical to those of the 1970s or 1980s, concerns over the representation of women remain prevalent. In the 2000s, the so-called Bechdel–Wallace test became deployed in public debates as a tool for measuring the representation and objectification of women. Named after Alison Bechdel who first presented the idea in her 1985 comic strip, "Dykes to Watch Out For", the test measures whether a popular representation, such as a film, has at least two female characters who have a conversation with each other about something other than a man. Just over 60 percent of contemporary films listed on bechdeltest.com have passed the test, in contrast to some 50 percent in the 1960s, suggesting that developments in gendered representation, even if measured in such simple and mechanistic ways, have been less than radical.

Similar findings are regularly made in studies by the Geena Davis Institute on Gender in Media that tracks gender bias in children's television programming, advertising and cinema internationally. According to the institute's analysis of the top hundred grossing animated and non-animated family films from 2007 to 2017, for example, male lead characters outnumbered female ones two to one (or 71.3 percent to 28.8 percent), with white leads outnumbering non-white ones one to four (See Jane, 2019a). The situation in the hundred highest grossing popular films was, in contrast, 60.9 percent versus 39.1 percent. According to another report, however, "female characters account for 36.2% of speaking time and 39.0% of screen time", they were "six times more likely than male characters to be shown in revealing clothing (27.3% compared to 4.6%)" (See Jane, 2019b). Without elaborating on the limitations and possibilities of the research methodology deployed, it would seem evident that sexist streaks continue to cut through popular cinematic representation, and that female bodies are offered as (silent) objects of visual pleasure much more frequently than male ones. This is intimately tied in with organizational cultures and the sets of values and views that they support or facilitate. The accounts of sexual harassment and abuse within media and film production, which have fuelled the #MeToo movement since October 2017 have shed light into some of these dynamics within Hollywood, and beyond, making evident sexism as an organizational practice that is accepted with smaller or larger degrees of silence.

The issues involved in the politics of representation are, then, broader than those focused on sexual depiction alone, leading us back to the question as to why critiques of objectification tend to cluster on instances of sexual depiction and arguments over sexualization rather than other concerns. While we elaborate on this in Chapter 3 by further exploring the radical feminist roots of objectification debates and their emphasis on pornographic representation in particular, we would like to note here that a focus on the sexual display of female bodies too frequently trumps contextual considerations, the context and political economy of the media production involved.

Symbolic struggle against hegemonic femininity

It should also be noted that, before the 1970s, feminist activism was focused on critiquing beauty standards and gender roles beyond sexual displays as such. Well before the publication of either Berger's television show or Mulvey's essay, feminist activists protested against the politics of gendered representation, extending their critiques to the beauty industry and the commodity markets attached to it. On 7 September 1968, feminists organized a demonstration against the Miss America 1969 contest held in Atlantic City, New Jersey. Attracting some 200 participants, the "No More Miss America" protest involved a picket, leafleting, as well as performative actions – releasing a stink bomb and crowning a sheep as beauty queen in protest against the perceived "cattle auction" and "beauty slavery" mentality of the pageant. Most famously, the protesters introduced a large "Freedom Trash Can" for the junking of objects connected to feminine grooming and female oppression, from bras to girdles, corsets, hairspray, false eyelashes, makeup, high-heel shoes, wigs, women's magazines, cleaning products and baby diapers (Redstockings, n.d.; Morgan and McNearney, 2018). Contrary to the stereotype of feminist bra-burners that the event sparked, no fires were lit.

The protest was organized by New York Radical Women, and initiated by Carole Hanisch, one of the activists connected to coining the immensely influential second-wave feminist slogan "the personal is political" in the very same year. Just as that slogan redefined the personal, the private, the individual, and the intimate as political, the protesters objected to the imperatives of feminine beauty – both in terms of the norms it creates and the mundane labour it requires. The organizers presented ten points of protest ranging from the pageant's racism to its consumerism, military ties, and overall ideology: "The pageant exercises Thought Control, attempts to sear the Image into our minds, to further make women oppressed and men oppressors; to enslave us all the more in high-heeled, low-status roles; to inculcate false values in young girls; to use women as beasts in buying; to seduce us to prostitute ourselves before our own oppression" (New York Radical Women, 1970: 588).

In a permit request, Robin Morgan – one of the group's activists particularly known for her 1974 anti-pornography feminist slogan, "porn is the theory, rape is the practice" – addressed the city mayor Richard S. Jackson with a description of the demonstration's rationale to "protest against the Miss America Pageant, which projects an image of women that many American women find unfortunate: the emphasis being on body rather than brains, on youth rather than maturity, and on commercialism rather than humanity" (Morgan, 1968). The demonstration was limited to female participants only and, as an attack against a national gender icon, Miss America, it remains a key symbolic event in US second-wave feminism. The protest involved a firm critique of female looked-at-ness à la Berger in women refusing to shape themselves to fit cultural templates of heterosexually desirable femininity. While the notion of objectification has retrospectively been introduced as key motivation and focus for the demonstration, and while this emphasis is obvious in the protesters' critiques of cattle auction mentality, the concept was not yet part of feminist vocabulary of the late 1960s.

By focusing on a feminist body politics, as symbolized by the objects discarded into the freedom trashcan, the project further paved the way for the reworking of the codes of femininity through what Alison Bartlett and Margaret Henderson identify as a "form of political dress, and political address" (Bartlett and Henderson, 2016: 163) within the second-wave feminist movement: "An adoption of working men's overalls and the rejection of bras aim to confound the dress codes of conventional femininity and illustrate the importance of practicality to feminist dress – a value that also works to reduce the sexual objectification of women. (...) They become a method with which to make the body a key signifier of feminist identity, propaganda, and allegiance".

The coding of conventionally feminine artefacts as "woman-garbage" has continued to be influential in activism around objec-tification; particularly where dress, display and sexual behaviour is concerned. In the 1990s, feminist Riot Grrrls took a more playful and provocative approach, wearing "little-girl dresses with Fredericks of Hollywood tacky glamour, rugged boots, small-town-American second-hand garments, and, especially in the USA, pro-minent tattoos or piercings" (Polhemus, 1994: 123), thereby mixing up and recirculating signs associated with children and adulthood, practicality and glamour, mainstream and alternative style, and drawing attention to "how genders are socially constructed" (Kearney, 1997: 221). The SlutWalk protests beginning in 2011 worked in a similar way to reclaim and question conventions of respectable dress, as well as words used to denigrate women's feminine and/or sexual behaviour – "slut" and "*cunt* and *queer* and *pussy* and *girl*" (Klein in Gillis and Munford, 2004: 171).

As we have shown in this chapter, body politics connected to cultural representation and self-representation alike have been central to feminist activism protesting against depictions of women as passive and silent objects of the male gaze both before and since the introduction of the notion of objectification into the feminist voca-bulary. Moving to address objectification head-on, Chapter 3 returns back to the question of why and how sex became such a key focus in feminist critiques of objectification and, by extension, in critiques of gendered representation. Examining the legacy of radi-cal feminist thought and activism in and for debates on objectifica-tion, we further expand on our critique of the analytical limitations of binary gender models while also considering how the boundaries of acceptable and unacceptable, normal and irregular sex have become drawn in feminist debate and analysis.

3 Radical feminism and the objectification of women

As we observed in Chapter 1, there are many different ways in which people can be objectified, many of these unrelated to sex. Bearing in mind Martha Nussbaum's broad unpacking of what objectification may mean, any kind of person can be objectified in the sense of being stripped of autonomy and volition, and being treated as an instrument for the gain of others: as in slavery, or trafficking for manual labour, for example. And yet in current public debates about objectification, the term is almost always applied to the ways that women are represented – objectification is seen, usually through a heterosexual framework, as something specifically pertaining to women, their social position and agency. And in those public debates, objectification is almost always related to sexualization, so that objectification is repeatedly collapsed with, and understood as referring to sexual objectification. In this chapter we ask why and how it has become the case that sexuality – and heterosexuality in particular – has remained the key terrain, and what does this mean for ways of understanding female sexual agency?

Critiques of gendered modes of seeing and the predominance of the male gaze, as examined in Chapter 2, focused on practices of object-making even before the notion of objectification gained ground in feminist critique as such. The development of objectification as a key term to understand gender relations was amplified by anti-pornography feminist activism and scholarship, and from the framework of radical feminist thought of writers such as Andrea Dworkin and Catharine MacKinnon in particular. According to a broader thread running through feminist critiques of objectification, pornography renders women as things, while things – that is, the products of pornography – are treated as human beings in that they come to define femininity and form relations according to which actual women are treated (see Langton, 2009: 2). In these articulations, pornography is seen as not merely a media genre but a social technology and ideological actor that produces false understandings concerning gender, sexuality and social equality, to detrimental effect. In order to understand what this means for how the notion of objectification continues to be deployed, this chapter takes a closer look at Dworkin's and MacKinnon's writings and the continuing legacy of radical feminism.

Into the binary

Debates about the objectification and commodification of women became prominent within feminist circles in the 1970s and 1980s, and feminist disputes about sex and sexuality began to take the form of "debates over pornography" (Segal, 1992: 11). The growing centrality of sexuality for feminist theory and activism during this period tended to privilege pornography as "*the* feminist issue of the 1980s" (Segal, 1992: 3), drawing together an emerging focus on sexual abuse, harassment, and violence as key issues in western second-wave feminism with a concern with the role of the media in the gendered politics of everyday life. Within English-speaking contexts in particular, pornography became "overburdened with significance" (Segal, 1992: 65), both as a way of talking about sex and as an emblem of misogyny. While there were a variety of feminist positions on pornography during this period, and while pornography was not seen as the most pressing concern in many local contexts, anti-pornography politics grew increasingly dominant within North America and elsewhere in the English-speaking world. From this position, pornography was seen as eroticizing the imbalance of power between men and women, its "characteristic reduction of women to passive, perpetually desiring bodies – or bits of bodies – eternally available for servicing men" (Segal, 1992: 2). Radical feminist authors presented a powerful and resonant account of the ideology of gender in society. In her *Pornography: Men Possessing Women*, originally published in 1981, Dworkin unequivocally identifies heterosexual sex as an expression and symbol of male supremacy:

The male ... forces the female to conform to his supremely ridiculously definition of her as sexual object. He fetishizes her body as a whole and in its parts ... In practice, fucking is an act of possession – simultaneously an act of ownership, taking, force; it is conquering; it expresses in intimacy power over and against, body to body, person to thing.

(Dworkin, 1989: 22–3)

Male heterosexual desire is, for Dworkin, premised on the objectification of women who, historically, have been understood (in law and practice) as the property of men: fathers and husbands. As chattel, or movable property, women have been located in the same category with "cattle (...), slaves, beasts of burden, domesticated animals" that are all valued and used as property, and as things (Dworkin, 1989: 101–2). More specifically, women have been, and remain, sexual property:

Male supremacy depends on the ability of men to view women as sexual objects, and deviations from this exercise of male power and female oblivion are discouraged.... The primary target of objectification is the woman. In male culture, men do argue about the proper bounds of objectification, especially about the viability of objectifying other males; but men do not argue about the moral meaning of objectification as such. It is taken for granted that a sexual response is an objectified response: that is, a response aroused by an object with specific attributes that in themselves provoke sexual desire.

(Dworkin, 1989: 113)

In this framework, which postulates male culture as monolithically uniform, women are categorically cast in the role of objects whose instrumental function is to sexually arouse men. MacKinnon, writing in a similarly binary and heteronormative framework, argues that:

the moulding, direction, and expression of sexuality organizes society into two sexes – women and men – which division underlies the totality of social relations. Sexuality is that social process which creates, organizes, expresses, and directs desire, creating the social beings we know as women and men, as their relations create society.

(MacKinnon, 1982: 516)

Patriarchy, it is argued, maps a whole series of qualities onto the male/female binary – male means active, strong – a subject; female means passive, weak – an object. For Dworkin (1988: 265), patriarchal ideology has "an ahistorical character – a sameness across time and cultures". Under such conditions of existence, all aspects of social and cultural life, and in particular gender roles and the subordinate status of women, are perpetuated through ideological positioning within which women are, literally and metaphorically, fucked. It then follows that sexuality becomes not only a realm of contestation, but also something of a battleground in a struggle for a more just society, one that must involve women's ownership of their own bodies and sexuality:

> that the personal is political means that gender as a division of power is discoverable and verifiable through women's intimate experience of sexual objectification, which is definitive of and synonymous with women's lives as gender female.
>
> (MacKinnon, 1982: 535)

Since heterosexuality is here premised on a fundamental gender imbalance and the oppression of women, female sexual desire, these writers argue, must necessarily involve a desire to be objectified, and to find pleasure in one's subservient, passive position – an argument not distant from, albeit not identical to, Mulvey's conceptualization of female film spectatorship as steeped in masochistic, passive pleasure in women's own objectification. Sexual objectification, as a form of alienation, is for MacKinnon the primary process of the subjection of women, one that "unites act with word, construction with expression, perception with enforcement, myth with reality. Man fucks woman; subject verb object" (MacKinnon, 1982: 541). Dworkin agrees: "The sex act" means penile intermission followed by penile thrusting, or fucking. The woman is acted on; the man acts and through action expresses sexual power, the power of masculinity. (Dworkin, 1989: 23)

There is not much agency possible, in this way of thinking, for women in patriarchal cultures, except for that involved in rendering oneself into an object of male desire. As heterosexuality is defined through male dominance and action, for Dworkin and MacKinnon women are simply left with the position of receptivity, reactivity and ultimate negativity – as soon as a woman in a patriarchal culture engages with sexuality, they argue, she becomes an object that is defined and controlled by men. Heterosexuality is here seen as a means of male control over female bodies that extends from the routines and structures of matrimony to symbolic representations foregrounding male perspectives and marginalizing female ones.

The issue, then, is not merely one of representation: it also that of sexual practices and politics in real life. While Dworkin, counter to common view, did not argue that all heterosexual penile penetration was rape, the threat of male violence was inbuilt in her conceptualization of heterosexuality – as in the index entry, "Penis, essential use of" in *Pornography: Men Possessing Women* (Dworkin, 1989). It was argued that porn served as a template for men's behaviour, as demonstrated in Robin Morgan's slogan "Pornography is the theory, and rape the practice." In addition to mapping out a correlation, or causality, between pornographic representation and sexual violence, Morgan expanded her discussion to male exploitation of life and resources on a global scale: "And what a practice. The violation of an individual woman is *the* metaphor for man's enforcing of himself on whole nations (rape as the crux of war), on nonhuman creatures (rape as the lust behind hunting and related carnage), and on the planet itself (reflected even in our own language – carving up 'virgin territory', with strip-mining often referred to as a 'rape of the land')" (Morgan, 1980: 139–40). As vernacular theory for this all, porn then came to stand as blueprint for the rape and destruction of not only female bodies, but also that of the Earth itself.

Many radical feminists, key figures such as Adrienne Rich and Kate Millett among them, embraced sexual pleasure in its woman-centric forms and argued for the necessity of developing an alternative erotic imaginary, and imagery, for challenging that which they saw as the sad and violent representational regime of heterosexual pornography. Second-wave feminism entailed a strong current of reclaiming female sexuality, from the 1970s manual Our Bodies, Ourselves (The Boston Women's Health Collective, 1973) celebrating women's selfknowledge and sexual agency to Nancy Friday's 1973 book, My Secret Garden detailing women's sexual fantasies, or Erica Jong's bestselling novel Fear of Flying of the same year chronicling female sexual self-discovery (Jong, 1973). However, a strand of radical separatist lesbianism argued that all heterosexual sex was necessarily oppressive and that women should take the feminist and political choice of lesbianism as a positive alternative to heterosexuality in the struggle against sexism (Krebs, 1987: 17). There was no necessity to take physical pleasure from sex with women, as feminists could, and perhaps also should, be "political lesbians" (Bindel, 2009).

These radical feminists have positioned sexual pleasure as something of problem to be resisted, as "woman's pleasure in sexual intercourse facilitated her subordination" (Jeffreys, 1990: 12). Women should be focusing on "social change, not simply individual self-fulfilment" (Russo, 1998: 34). These authors have critiqued "the obsession with masturbation and orgasm" (Jeffreys, 1990: 237) in second-wave feminism, noting that "what feels good is constructed by sexual oppression" (Cole, 1992: 131) and asking "[i]s an orgasm worth all of this self-annihilation?" (Cole, 1992: 130). Indeed, for Sheila Jeffreys (1990: 304), "[t]he absence of orgasm might more appropriately be seen as a form of resistance" against heterosexual patriarchy. These authors do not, however, offer an alternative model for a non-patriarchal sexuality. They demand "a total transformation of the way 'sex' is learned and experienced" (Jeffreys, 1992: 15) yet note that they cannot offer that alternative because "a world of freedom beyond heterosexuality cannot be envisaged" (Jeffreys, 1990: 4):

> We have a long way to go before we uncover the full extent of the damage. We may not see the full repair in our lifetimes and it may not be possible to chart the entire course for change. In my own travels I am constantly asked to reel off the full agenda. I cannot do that.
>
> (Cole, 1992: 132)

A feminist political agenda that is unable to offer alternatives to how gender and sexuality are envisioned comes with obvious limitations. It seems to us that a model which cannot suggest ways in which women can be sexual without becoming objects is neither empirically nor politically useful. Just as it is important to account for the diversity of approaches to female sexual agency and pleasure within radical feminism, it needs be noted that challenges to totalizing models of patriarchal sexuality articulated from other conceptual and theoretical viewpoints have been equally present in feminist thought across decades. The 1982 conference on Sexuality held at Barnard College, New York, marks a particular crossroads in feminist debates on sexuality. The conference and the publication that emerged from it (Vance, 1984b) are often cited as a key point in the emergence of a feminist "sex wars" waged throughout the 1980s in the United States in particular (Basiliere, 2009). The conference set out to pursue the complexity of sexual issues for women, both as "a domain of restriction, repression, and danger as well as a domain of exploration, pleasure, and agency" (Vance, 1984a: 1). Taking a more expansive view of sexual dangers than that espoused by writers such as Dworkin who foregrounded "violence, brutality, and coercion, in the form of rape, forcible incest, and exploitation, as well as everyday cruelty and humiliation" (ibid), the conference instead addressed the possibilities of sexual pleasures – including "explorations of the body, curiosity, intimacy, sensuality, adventure, excitement, human connection, basking in the infantile and non-rational" (ibid.)

The Barnard conference was strongly attacked by self-named radical feminists, and riven by passionate disagreements about whether BDSM – B/D (Bondage and Discipline), D/s (Dominance and submission), S/M (Sadism and Masochism) – could ever be feminist. The "Coalition for a Feminist Sexuality and Against Sadomasochism" picketed the event, handing out leaflets which denounced sadomasochism as a "reactionary, patriarchal sexuality" (Coalition for a Feminist Sexuality and Against Sadomasochism, 1983: 180). In particular, the Coalition attempted to speak to sadomasochistic lesbians:

> This coalition is not criticizing any women for ... having sadomasochistic fantasies, or for becoming sexually aroused by pornography. We acknowledge that all people who have been

socialized in patriarchal society – feminists and nonfeminists, lesbians and heterosexuals – have internalized its sexual patterns of dominance and submission. But ... [BDSM lesbians] are not acknowledging having internalized patriarchal messages and values. Instead, they are denying that these values are patriarchal.
(Coalition for a Feminist Sexuality and Against Sadomasochism, 1983: 181–2)

This question about whether BDSM practices are necessarily patriarchal – and thus, whether any woman who enjoys BDSM practices is failing to demonstrate actual sexual agency – has never quite gone away. Debates over BDSM, accused like porn of glorifying "unequal relations of power fundamental to a patriarchal society" (Bronstein, 2011: 285) have remained a divisive fault line in feminist debates for decades since. At the Barnard conference, Gayle Rubin analyzed a normative sexual hierarchy that she saw operating in Western society, a hierarchy that separates "good, normal, natural, blessed sexuality" from "bad, abnormal, unnatural, damned sexuality" (Rubin, 1984: 281). Within this model, the "charmed circle" of what society sees as good sexuality involves marital, heterosexual, monogamous relationships whereas pornography, along with promiscuous, kinky, casual, non-procreative and gay sex come to occupy the role of the bad. Rubin's analysis challenges this hierarchy and explains how certain sexual preferences and practices – as well as the bodies performing them – are cast as normal while others, such as BDSM practices, come to stand for morally corrupt freakiness. Her essay has been highly influential in both feminist studies of sexuality and in queer theory questioning the establishment of gendered and sexual norms.

The continuing appeal of radical feminist thought

Studying the work of Dworkin in particular is useful not just for helping us understand how the concept of objectification became a central part of feminist projects over the last four decades – it also helps us to see why this approach to thinking about gender relations remains so powerful and compelling today. The excerpts from Dworkin's work that we have quoted in this chapter make evident some of the affective appeal of her blunt, passionate and angry authorial voice (Paasonen, 2018; Smith and Attwood, 2013). There has in fact recently been renewed interest in her work, to the point that this can be considered something of a revival. Writing on *Last Days at Hot Slit* (Fateman and Scholder, 2019), a collection of Dworkin's previously published and unpublished work, Nona Willis Aronowitz (2019) positions herself as having grown up in the pro-sex 1990s feminist discourse where the so-called sex wars had already been fought, and not having had much appreciation for Dworkin. Yet she finds new urgency and resonance to Dworkin's writing in a cultural moment characterized by #MeToo and Donald Trump's presidency:

> We understand the need for a world that condemns male dom-ination while also taking female sexuality seriously – and still a harmonious blend of those two things eludes us … That's why the predation of powerful men, the slut-shaming of their vic-tims, and the avalanche of abortion restrictions … make us more pissed off than ever. … Next to the vacant, rah-rah ver-sion of sex positivity I grew up with in the '90s, Dworkin's rage seems downright clear-eyed.
>
> (Aronowitz, 2019: np)

There seems, then, to be – four decades later and in a drastically different cultural moment – a specific appeal to Dworkin's emo-tional prose, her fury at the way things are, the firmness of her political stance, and the fact that it allows for little ambiguity. Her work offers a strong, even all-encompassing, theory of heterosexual desire and male domination through the concept of objectification, and this can be compelling in the clarity that its binary logic enables. When we talk about a "strong theory", we are following the thinking of queer theorist Eve Kosofsky Sedgwick (2003) who uses that phrase to describe forms of cultural inquiry that both offer and necessitate unambiguous results. For Sedgwick (2003: 133), strong theories are firm in their premises and in their commitment to the destabilization of the operations of power that they presume and identify. There is however the danger that such approaches are also potentially totalizing in their outcomes. This form of inter-pretation is focused on uncovering the hidden workings of power that have in fact always been known, and postulated, from the very beginning (Sedgwick, 2003: 130). In other words, with strong theory there is no process of uncovering evidence – you know what needs to be proved before you start gathering your data (should you, in fact, be interested in gathering any), so there is no possibility that an hypothesis will ever be disproved. Evidence that doesn't seem to support the hypothesis will be dismissed, ignored, or interpreted in such a way that it can be argued to support the hypothesis, even if it doesn't.

This is, in fact, also the logic of conspiracy theories and "fake news", where the absence of evidence is, in itself, proof of the hypothesis, because it reveals how powerful the "deep state" is, and how it has destroyed the evidence that must have existed. Such an approach to interpretation risks being both generalizing and tautological in that it can only ever "prove the very same assumptions with which it began" (Sedgwick, 2003: 135). Strong theory is decidedly useful for activism in that it both identifies social problems and offers solutions to them. At the same time, the seeming clarity it involves comes at the expense of accounting for ambiguities, complexities and contextual nuances. There are, then, risks to the seductions of strong theory that orders the world into clear-cut categories, drawn along the axis of binary gender.

The allure of this strong theory is nevertheless obvious in the clarity that it affords. For example, the opinion columnist Michelle Goldberg applauds the emotional force and poignancy of Dworkin's writing, detailing her personal experiences of violence and abuse within marriage and beyond:

> So what is it in Dworkin's long-neglected oeuvre that has suddenly become resonant? ... Dworkin, so profoundly out of fashion just a few years ago, suddenly seems prophetic. "Our enemies – rapists and their defenders – not only go unpunished; they remain influential arbiters of morality; they have high and esteemed places in the society; they are priests, lawyers, judges, lawmakers, politicians, doctors, artists, corporation executives, psychiatrists and teachers," Dworkin said in a lecture she wrote in 1975, included in "Last Days at Hot Slit." Maybe this once sounded paranoid. After Trump's election, the Brett Kavanaugh hearings, and revelations of predation by men including Roger Ailes, Harvey Weinstein, Les Moonves, Larry Nassar and countless figures in the Catholic Church, her words seem

frighteningly perceptive. ... Indeed, some of Dworkin's ideas have been reincarnated in #MeToo, and not just because she also sought to challenge oppression by going public with her own stories of sexual abuse ... the renewed interest in Dworkin is a sign that for many women, our libidinous culture feels neither pleasurable nor liberating.

(Goldberg, 2019: np)

As a viral Twitter and Facebook campaign, the #MeToo movement has been predominantly concerned with heterosexual encounters, and focused attention on mundane sexual harassment, abuse, and violence targeted at, and experienced by, women. As such, it has been highly influential in pushing sexual harassment into a topic of public debate, resulting in careers being ruptured, individuals being sued, and generating new policies. Despite accounts of sexual violence targeted at men from people of different genders that have also emerged in discussions connected to the hashtag, #MeToo has nevertheless continued to centre on the abuse and discrimination of women by men. In this sense, it both builds on, and reproduces, a normative binary division between aggressive, even predatory, male sexual desire and its passive, vulnerable feminine recipients (Ringrose and Lawrence, 2018: 697; Sundén and Paasonen, 2019). #MeToo is about things done to women; that which women do, and why, has tended to be a lesser concern. This logic is appealing in its easy-to-digest form, doing away with the complexities involved in women being committed to sexist practices, or sexually assaulting other people, for example. Importantly, #MeToo has re-energized an altercation within feminism, one that Arlene Stein (2006) already considered as being only of historical relevance, namely that between feminists opposed to pornography, commercial sex and kink, and those arguing for a more complex view of sexual desire and agency: the divisions of sex wars as drawn along the lines of radical feminism versus feminists variously identifying as sex-positive, kinky or queer, in short, continue to hold power in the present.

This is evident in how the concept of patriarchy, all but absent from feminist vocabulary since the 1990s, has made a rhetorical comeback in the aftermath of #MeToo. Popularized in second-wave feminism, and central to radical feminist critique, patriarchy refers to a social system of male domination where men hold political and religious power and authority, and which, as an ideology, naturalizes gender inequalities and the oppression of women. In feminist debates, the notion of patriarchy has been critiqued for its ahistorical, generalizing tendencies not allowing for contextual differences in social structures and relations across time and space (see Walby, 1989). As Vrushali Patil points out, applying the concept of "patriarchy" to analyze gender relations results in, and represents "homogenous, monolithic accounts of gender oppression" (Patil, 2013: 847). Despite such limitations the concept – very much like that of objectification – retains a contemporary allure as shorthand for structural gendered inequalities. From this perspective, sexist views, actions or depictions are diverse and ubiquitous, yet connected by an overall ideology, according to which women are considered to be of lesser value.

The notion of patriarchy then makes it possible to connect such articulations and instances of sexism into a larger entity, or structure, that also lends them an unchanging status. We argue that it is necessary to pay attention both to similarity and difference in thinking about gender-based oppression. It is important that we see the structural issues that link disparate actions that oppress women; while at the same time we must understand that transformations during the past century in legal status pertaining to gender, class and race, including political rights and legal autonomy, show us that social hierarchies are by no means set or uncontested. Even if Western societies remain in many ways structured to disadvantage women, many social, economic, political and personal changes have been made. Things are not the same as they were fifty years ago when second-wave feminism was making its breakthrough, and many of those changes were achieved through those very political protests and social critiques.

OBJECT!

The risks of taking a binary approach that refuses to acknowledge differences, insisting that all men are a homogenous group of oppressors while women are an equally homogenous group objectified by men, can be seen in the development of a vigorous anti-trans strand of radical feminism. Here, the activities of the UK-based feminist group "OBJECT! Women Not Sex Objects" and their development since 2004 serves as a particularly pertinent example (see Figure 3.1). OBJECT!'s politics are deeply tied to the critique of objectification which have, over a decade and a half, moved in multiple directions.

Figure 3.1 OBJECT! website, March 2020

Founded to fight against the objectification of women in commercial media, OBJECT! started out by calling for newsagents and supermarkets to take responsibility for the sexist magazines that were on public display in their premises. For OBJECT!, representations of women's bodies were necessarily more problematic than representations of men's bodies. At a 2010 network launch event "What is the sexualisation of culture?" at the University of London, activists from the group complained against recurring critiques of their actions, where opponents argued that *Men's Health* objectifies men inasmuch as *Maxim* objectifies women and should hence be equally targeted as objects of critique. This critique was, of course, logically true in the sense that both magazines display semi-naked bodies as objects for fascinated and titillated viewing, yet one that the activists found irritating in deliberately missing the point of their action. The critique was also predictable in that, as we have argued, the concept of objectification, as it is commonly applied in public debates, struggles to account for gendered differences, or sexuality, in representational practices as such.

The key difference between these two kinds of magazines – ones targeted at men featuring photos of women and others featuring men – concern the ways in which male and female bodies are rendered objects of visual consumption. This difference, again, is simply too general for the notion of objectification, once mapped onto the model of binary gender, to productively tackle. The differences involved concern the power differentials afforded to various representations of bodies, as drawn along the axes of gender, age, fitness and race, bringing us back to a multitude of social hierarchies and their mundane reproduction in representational practices. While these can be reduced to a gender binary, such a framing truncates the complexity of issues at stake. Although the distinction between objecting to the objectification of women and objecting to sexism may seem minutely academic to some, we argue that it is in fact a crucial one in that the first involves the conditions of representation – depicting something or someone as something – while the latter is a question of discrimination and social relations of power, issues addressed in Chapter 2.

After a hiatus of some years, and with the invitation of activists Sheila Jeffreys and Heather Brunskell-Evans to the management board, OBJECT! became active on social media in 2018. On Twitter and Facebook, OBJECT! continues to object to airbrushed commercials, homophobia, commercial sex and transformations in UK obscenity legislation lifting bans on some forms of pornography and the consensual sexual acts connected to, and represented in, them. However, the bulk of OBJECT!'s activities have shifted to objecting to trans rights, effectively redefining OBJECT! from a radical feminist to a trans-exclusionary radical feminist (TERF) group promoting "women's sex-based human rights, which affirms that the discrimination and oppression of women all over the world is based upon biological sex, and not the postmodern concept of 'gender identity'" (OBJECT!, 2019; also Hines, 2019).

Their activism is a reaction to the increasingly visibility of trans people in Western countries. A variety of research disciplines from psychiatry through to queer studies have highlighted how, from the moment a child is born, behaviour is reinforced and/or discouraged in order to reproduce prescribed gender performance (de Beauvoir, 2011 [1949] to Stoller, 1968 to Butler, 2002). Throughout the early twentieth century trans people were studied by the medical and psychological disciplines, and it was not until the 1990s that transgender studies emerged as an academic field more widely, and particularly in the humanities and social sciences. Sandy Stone's 1991 essay, "The Empire Strikes Back: A Post-transsexual Manifesto", critiquing feminist understandings of trans as forms of false consciousness and out of date gender stereotypes (Stryker, 2006: 4) was particularly influential to the emergent field of trans studies, which has continued to take shape through platforms such as the journal, *TSQ: Transgender Studies Quarterly*, published by Duke University Press since 2014. Stephen Whittle (2006: xii) credits this new scholarship as allowing trans people to "reclaim the reality of their bodies", and to change theorizations concerning gender itself.

Many radical feminists oppose this development. For its part, OBJECT! objects to gendered self-identification, foregrounding instead the bodies that people are born into and the need to resist gender-based stereotyping. According to their line of argumentation, trans people are trapped in gender stereotypes, unable to live out their lives satisfactorily within their narrow confines without resorting to practices that the group openly describes as bodily self-mutilation. This does not mean that the group sees trans people as victims of gender stereotyping in the sense of lacking in agency, rather, OBJECT! associates a malicious kind of agency with transmen and transwomen alike. The group shares links to articles on child abuse and sexual violence committed by trans people who, consequently, become figures of threat (Vähäpassi, 2019). In understanding transwomen as men, and as actors promoting the very male definitions of women and femininity that feminists have, through critiques of objectification, resisted, TERFs are opposed to transwomen's access to women-only spaces, from gender-segregated bathrooms to changing rooms and separatist communities. Transgender more broadly emerges as a violent force adding to the discrimination of women by violating women-only spaces and infiltrating feminist politics: "We OBJECT to the transcult. Biology rules." (Facebook, 15 January 2019).

United by a common enemy, trans-exclusionary feminists have recently joined forces with conservative lobbyists heralding binary gender models based on biology (e.g. Greenesmith, 2019; Little, 2019). A historical parallel can be drawn to the alliances between radical feminists (such as Dworkin and MacKinnon) and Christian coalitions jointly fighting pornography during the Reagan presidency (Segal, 1993; Vance, 1997). These strategic alliances between feminist activism and moral conservative political agendas involve drastically different, in fact incompatible, political stakes concerning gender equality and women's rights, yet similar goals when it comes to explicit media representations of sex. In the course of such alliances, heteronormative and sexist views on gendered agency and sexual depiction, paradoxically, find support in feminist activism dedicated to fight precisely such agendas and views. This alliance affords feminist activism broader public visibility and resonance, yet these come at the expense of aligning with repressive, regressive and harmful politics concerning both gender and sexuality. The effects of such alliances are, from a feminist standpoint, unpredictable and questionable, as evidenced by lesbian BDSM porn being among the first materials to be targeted under Reagan through the joint efforts of feminists and conservative politicians (Rubin, 1995).

The leap that OBJECT! has taken, from critiquing lads' mags, advertising and pornography to resisting and attacking trans rights, may seem surprising at first glance. Considered more closely, it can be seen to follow logically from the binary gender model upon which radical feminist theory and activism build, and this is the key reason why we are addressing the group's activities at length here. Within this logic, men are subjects, women objects. While radical feminism resists gender stereotyping and narrow ways of being female (or male), it remains committed to gender as a binary, biological structure where, under patriarchal ideology, men hold and execute power over women, independent of how individual women may understand their own ways of being. The category of woman, as construed in radical feminist thought, is then incompatible with transwomen whose presence in women-only spaces was previously contested, and remains so to date (see Williams, 2016; O'Keefe, 2016; also Goldberg, 2014). Identifying the current media visibility of trans people as well as legal transformations in trans rights – as exemplified by anti-discrimination bills – as something akin to a cult, or even an epidemic, trans-exclusive feminists clearly see trans folk and their rights as eating away at the very foundations of feminist politics and, ultimately, as amounting to an attack on the rights of women.

The complexity and multiplicity of identities has generally not been a key concern in radical feminist thought that has been cut through by a firmly binary gender logic. At the same time, it is important to point out that Dworkin's and MacKinnon's work was not trans-exclusionary, and that not all radical feminism should be identified as TERF, either historically or in a contemporary framework. The trans question has indeed divided radical feminism since the 1970s, with high-profile activists such as Robin Morgan and lesbian separatists in particular resisting trans-inclusivity and refusing to use the gender pronouns preferred by trans people. Unpacking these tensions,

Cameron Awkward-Rich (2017: 829), points out the interconnection of anti-pornography feminism and TERF activism, as represented by Sheila Jeffreys, whose *Gender Hurts: A Feminist Analysis of Trans-genderism* strongly argues against the inclusion of trans women in feminist separatist spaces (Jeffreys, 2014). The strong theory upon which radical feminist critiques of the objectification of women – seen as crystallized in heterosexual pornography – builds on the premise of binary, biological gender.

The complexity of differences

We have tried to lay out this argument as fairly as possible but we do not agree with it. It is our argument that feminist critique and acti-vism cannot stick to, or hark back to, the kind of binary logic that structured influential, classic accounts of objectification composed in the 1970s and 1980s. Such an approach ignores decades of feminist, queer and postcolonial scholarship by women from diverse racial and class backgrounds that has challenged binary understandings of gender and sexual desire, and foregrounded the complex inter-sectionality of social hierarchies and relations of power while paying close attention to the materiality of bodies. Kimberle Crenshaw coined the notion of intersectionality to refer to the range of distinct factors that contribute to systems of inequality and oppression that include gender. She notes that an intersectional approach is necessary because "the problem with identity politics is not that it fails to transcend difference, as some critics charge, but rather the opposite – that it frequently conflates or ignores intragroup differences" (Cren-shaw, 1991: 1242). A primary focus on gender as an identity category and an axis of power risks effacing from view other differences that matter, press upon people in different ways, and impact people's possibilities to act – the problem merely amplifies if gender is under-stood as innate and immutable, as in TERF activism.

As intersectional theory notes, we cannot presume that women form a single group with shared political goals. For example, the majority of white women in the United States who voted in the 2016 presidential election voted for Donald Trump, despite his clear and explicitly sexist views and anti-feminist politics; while the vast majority of Black male voters who did so for Hillary Clinton (Jaffe, 2018). In that context, it is clear that a political approach which argues that any woman is automatically more of a political ally in a feminist struggle than any man needs to be challenged. Similarly, according to available data, sexual abuse and harassment do not merely concern women but are disproportionally directed against sexual minorities, trans and gender-queer people, Indigenous populations, as well as people with disabilities. This means that focusing on the axis of gender alone risks ignoring the multi-dimensional specificities of sexual harassment and abuse. It can also mean presenting the experiences of straight, white, middle-class women as universal, truncating the potential avenues that feminist activism can take and, consequently, the social impact that it can have.

In this chapter we have explored radical feminist writing about gendered ideologies in society, which present men as agents and women as objects. This ideology is understood to operate in a variety of ways, including social expectations about behaviour, stereotypes about roles, institutions such as marriage, and particularly through the practice of sex. Dworkin and MacKinnon both saw heterosexual power dynamics encapsulated in the eroticization of gendered power differentials within the realm of sexuality. For them this included the practices of sex in real life as well as in representation, pornography in particular being a central symbol of female objectification. Building on the legacy of entwining critiques of objectification with those concerning pornography in radical feminist thought, in Chapter 4, we shift our focus from the politics of representation to the realm of sex work in order to further unravel the complexities that the concepts of subjects and objects in debates over objectification involve.

4   Sex objects and sexual subjects

According to a radical feminist stance addressed in Chapter 3 – and also shared by some not identifying as radical feminist – the act of producing pornography objectifies the women involved while the consumption of pornography further feeds a toxic gender dynamic (e. g. McKinnon and Dworkin, 1998). This approach insists that all kinds of sex work, pornography included, are a form of gender-based exploitation rather than labour, and function as a site where women are turned into "things" and made to "sell themselves". Radical feminists have rejected the term "sex worker" that is preferred by people who do this work to describe themselves, because it suggests active control over their labour. They insist on using the term "prostitute" – or "prostituted women" (Busch et al, 2002) – instead, arguing that the women involved in sex work are not acting out of their own knowing or free volition. Dworkin's definition of pornography as "the graphic depiction of women as vile whores" existing "only within a framework of male sexual domination" (Dworkin, 1999: 200) certainly came with an added degree of emotional charge and judgement.

The overall understanding of pornography as a form of violence involving the objectification of women has gradually come to underpin less politically articulated discussions and analyses in a range of settings. Increasingly, porn has been presented, not just as a metaphor for violence, but as a template or even an instruction manual for harmful sexual behaviour. In connection with this, the idea of making pornography as being innately objectifying of women has grown common in activism and public debate. In this chapter, we examine both these debates and the work and public figure of Jiz Lee, self-defined as "queer genderqueer gender-variant trans fag androgynous erotic model pornstar dykestar sex worker artist activist instigator sweetheart lover polyamorous non-monogymous hippie punk leftist past-vegan sex positive nympho slut dyke darling juicy geek" (Lee, in King is a Fink, 2010). The aims of the chapter are manifold: to lay out the stakes and issues involved in conceptualizing sex workers as objects (or at least as objectified); to tease out complexities in how the work of pornography work is practiced and understood; and to explore how sexual subjectivity and objectification in pornography can be made sense of and how norms concerning appropriate or "good" sex play into all this.

Bodily work

In the United States, the "Fight Online Sex Trafficking Act" and the "Stop Enabling Sex Trafficking Act" (FOSTA-SESTA) came into effect in 2018, making social media services responsible for online trafficking should they allow for discussions of sex work or any advertisements connected to such services. This has concretely limited the possibilities of sex workers to organize and communicate on online platforms and, in doing so, to make their own work safer (see Paasonen, Jarrett and Light, 2019). Although specific to the United States, the legislation has global resonances as any online company wishing to operate in the country, independent of where its corporate headquarters are based, needs to comply with it. Similarly, pornography has been defined as a "public health crisis" in twelve US states (at the time of writing), and the formulation remains central to contemporary anti-pornography activism defining online pornography as unprecedentedly harmful and dangerous. These attempts to regulate and to possibly ban porn also claim to foreground the safety of sex workers. But they largely ignore what sex workers say about their experiences.

Concerns about sex work as objectification are often presented as based on a concern for sex workers, yet it is notable that most sex workers disagree with this perspective. Contemporary anti-sex work initiatives commonly conflate sex work with sex trafficking, arguing that all sex work is a form of exploitation, casting sex workers as victims or as otherwise lacking in agency. The radical feminist perspective that all sex work is objectifying depends in part on an undervaluing of work that foregrounds the body (Cahill, 2014), especially in the context of sex. Meanwhile, other forms of labour that involve attending to the bodies of people who pay for services – not least childcare, nursing, hairdressing, massage and so on equally performed by women (see Ehrenreich and Hochschild, 2003; Wolkowitz et al, 2013) – are not seen as objectifying and demeaning to the same extent, even as these occupations belong to the low-wage sector. This line of thinking singles out sex work from other forms of body work in assuming that, in sex work, a person becomes entirely "reduced" to their body, even as performing such work successfully "requires workers to function precisely as subjects (beings with emotions, desires, and sensations)" (Cahill, 2011: 842).

This rejection of sex work as work is further underpinned by the idea that selling sex involves "selling the self", suggesting that human intimacy should be separate from labour and consumption as something not "for sale" (as the title of Christine Stark and Rebecca Whisnant's collection in 2004 puts it). Yet a focus on sex work as being particularly problematic because it commercializes human relations ignores "the fact that all facets of our lives are commercialized to some extent" (Lee and Sullivan, 2016: 107); that postindustrial economies are increasingly marked by a "prolifera-tion of forms of service work" that reconfigure commerce and inti-macy, love and labour (Bernstein, 2007: 6); and that both financial arrangements, rights and responsibilities and various forms of reproductive labour have always been key to the institution of marriage as key arena of socially accepted intimacy (Zelizer, 2005).

As sex work is refused status as work, it becomes seen as a realm of exploitation and oppression instead. This means denouncing the agency of women performing such work (that is not work) as objects lacking in actual volition. Ariel Levy's view is extreme, but not untypical of this approach, according to which the exchange of money objectifies and hence dehumanizes the one receiving compensation for their efforts:

> strippers, porn stars, pinups ... *aren't even people.* They are merely sexual personae, erotic dollies from the land of make-believe ... As far as we know, they have no ideas, no feelings, no political beliefs, no relationships, no past, no future, no *humanity.*
> (Levy, 2005: 196, emphasis in the original)

Approaches like this not only fail to engage with the complexities of these shifts, but entirely strip sex workers of their capacity to think, feel, act as political agents, form bonds with others or, indeed, be fully human. This line of argumentation, which sees sex workers as sexual objects, effectively strips them of agency and volition while obviously failing to account for their own views, perspectives, experiences and concerns.

Now, consider the photograph of Jiz Lee in Figure 4.1.

Figure 4.1 Jiz Lee suspended.
Photo courtesy of The Dark Arts

On the one hand, Lee (preferred pronouns they/them) is naked, tied up and has very limited mobility. They are offered as objects of vision to be examined, and possibly sexually desired. On the other hand, there is little that is passive to their display of the self. Lee's body is athletic, their gaze firm and their position – against all odds – comes across as active, even determined. The photograph can function as a pornographic object. But is Lee themself an object?

Lee has been working in porn for over a decade, appearing in more than two hundred projects from independent erotic films to hardcore gonzo pornography (Lee, 2019). They are also a triathlete and creator of "International Fisting Day" and, through their Karma Pervs project that uses porn to raise money for queer communities, they are active in the world of philanthropy while also serving on boards for community arts organizations (King is a Fink, 2010). They write about their experiences in porn both in mainstream books (Lee, 2015) and academic publications (Lee, 2013) – which they also edit (Lee and Sullivan, 2016). Lee lectures at universities across America and has also appeared in the hit Amazon TV series *Transparent* (2014–2019).

The kind of pornography that Lee appears in can be rough and edgy, involving BDSM, including electricity play. In addition to watching Lee having sex – often aggressive kinky sex – onscreen, we can also read about their experiences with pornography:

> Porn is an extension of my own sexual expression, a blend of art and documentation ... I learn a lot about myself when I do porn. It provided a space for me to explore BDSM through bondage and electricity. Porn has become part of how I practice being poly; shoots are a clearly defined container offering distinct boundaries where I can have sex with close friends on preestablished terms. Porn is part of my exhibitionism and a place where I can literally own my sexuality. Performative sex is thrilling, and with sober sets, regular STI testing and a crew of professionals, I've had the opportunity to explore the vast edges of my sexuality, gender and fantasy. Some of the safest and most satisfying sex I've had has happened on camera. I've had so many positive experiences in porn that I'm convinced it's one of the best decisions I've ever made.
>
> (Lee, 2015: np)

They write about the times when they said no to pornographers:

> Once I was booked to work with a mainstream company and two days before the shoot, the producer found out I usually shoot while "naturally hairy". I was told immediately that I was required to shave everything for the scene. My choice in that situation was to decline the shoot.
>
> (Lee, 2013: 276–7)

And they write that they are:

> humbled that my very existence in porn brings visibility to the simple fact that queer and gender-variant people are deserving of a happy and healthy sexuality ... I'm working with friends and lovers to create images of intimacy, trust and pleasure. And we're having fun! That is what porn means to me.
>
> (Lee, 2015: np)

It seems to us that Jiz Lee acts as a kind of limit case for thinking about sexual subjectivity in a patriarchal culture. Lee is not driven to work in porn by financial desperation but "can afford to not work with people I'm not interested in" (in King is a Fink, 2010). They have a university education, they are an artist, they earn money through forms of work that are not sex work. They are consistently clear that they are aware of the structured inequalities of the society in which they live:

> We write at a time when sexual knowledge is typically buried in shame, fear and ignorance. Where hate crimes against people whose gender and sexual expression differ from a strictly defined template are alarming statistics; the suicide and murder of trans women of color in particular are screaming indicators that something in our understanding of sex and gender is clearly amiss. If our experiences of sexual stigma and its intersections are any indicator of the social inequality of our time, may our words be stepping-stones for increased sexual awareness and nuances to come.
>
> (Lee, 2015: np)

They talk and write about their reasons for doing porn:

> I feel that my audience identifies with me as we are people from marginalized communities with limited representation in pornography and what representation there is aids in sexual empowerment, validation of sexual orientation and gender expression, and sexual education. Things not seen in Hollywood, things not taught in Sex Ed. Things not seen most places, period. In short, the product we are making is a profoundly intimate reflection of our lives.
>
> (Lee, in King is a Fink, 2010: np)

They work with ethically conscientious production companies. The CrashPad series on which Jiz Lee started their pornography career in 2005 is cited by researchers as an example of "fair trade", ethical porn (Mondin, 2014: 190) that "breaks with the heteronormative and often sexist traditions of the genre" (Schorn, 2012: 22), presenting "complex explorations of identity and metatextual gestures" (Beirne, 2012: 230). It is one of the examples given by Mireille Miller-Young when she writes that "If we look … at pornography created by black women … we see erotic expression that is much more creative and pleasurable than many critics might suspect" (Miller-Young, 2010: 223). Shine Louise Houston – the queer woman of colour who created and runs the series – has commented on her desire to create "well-made lesbian porn … people from our community representing our community" (Bonilla, 2019: np) as well as a new, healthy business model involving equal flat rate for all performers (Houston, in Brocart, 2014: np). Houston also aims to support the sexual agency of performers: "I'm usually asking them what they would like to do. My style is to follow them … I come in, I have no idea of what's going to happen and I'm like 'what do you guys want to do?'. Sometimes they have an idea, sometimes they don't. Sometimes they tell me 'we're going to do this' and I tell them 'we may do something else'" (Houston, in Brocart, 2014: np).

Jiz Lee is sexual. Jiz Lee is sexy. Jiz Lee performs their sex in public. But Jiz Lee clearly cannot be reduced to a sex object – that is, something or someone serving an instrumental purpose for others rather than someone enacting subjectivity in their work or actions. Is Jiz Lee not a sexual subject? If we cannot agree that they have sexual agency, then who does?

The complexities of sexual agency

As will be apparent from the previous chapters of this book, for many activists there is no possibility of women having sexual agency in a patriarchal culture, let alone for women – or those identified as women – to enact sexual agency when performing in pornography as objects of the male gaze. For those writers, it does not matter if women make the choice (which, in their understanding, would not be a choice at all) to perform their sexuality in an exhibitionist way, as it is impossible to have genuine choice in patriarchal culture. They argue that when women say that they are making a choice to work in porn "we may often suspect that a level of denial is operative" (Whisnant, 2004: 24). Radical feminist writer Taylor Lee argues that:

> Women in the sex industry frequently display selective memory or some type of mental block. The purpose of the denial is to protect oneself from painful experiences like rape or abuse and/ or from looking at some of one's behaviors, like having sex with strangers and pretending to enjoy it.
>
> (Taylor Lee, 2004: 58)

For these writers, women may think that they are taking control of their sexuality, but it's really "dissociation" (Taylor Lee, 2004: 59), "delusion", "manipulation", "coercion" (Taylor Lee, 2004: 62), that it is not "genuine consent" (Clarke, 2004: 204), that it is "internalised misogyny" (Stark, 2004: 289) and that these women are "dupes" (Stark, 2004: 290), "desperate, addicted to drugs" (Smith, in Simonton and Smith, 2004: 354), that they have "post-traumatic stress disorder" and that they are " in denial" (Simonton and Smith, 2004: 355; Taylor Lee, 2004: 59). According to this "damaged goods" hypothesis, women end up having careers in porn as the result of childhood abuse and trauma, rather than through knowing choice, and of being under the power of the male-dominated adult industry during their careers. Such understanding is categorical and allows for no contextual nuance between different professionals, work cultures or regional cultures. Despite the myth being countered and refuted in empirical inquiry among porn performers (Griffith et al, 2013), it continues to hold much power and remains efficient in downplaying the agency and experiences of the women involved.

As we noted in Chapter 3, the feminist sex wars of the 1980s represent a fundamental split in feminist thinking about the possibility of sexual agency, and one that can never be fundamentally proved one way or the other. Is a woman's sexual agency genuine or deluded by patriarchal ideology? The question of whether a choice is genuine or not is one that belongs to that category of philosophical questions that can never be answered factually – they are, rather, questions of attitude and opinion. When people disagree about facts, these can be checked; but when people disagree about attitudes towards facts, that can't be so easily done. There are three broad kinds of attitudinal disagreements: disagreement about the importance of things (is this important?); disagreement about the value of things (is this good?) and disagreement about the reality of things (is this genuine?), none of which can be answered by a simple appeal to facts (McKee, 2005: 18). We cannot *prove* that Jiz Lee's choice to work in pornography is genuine – we cannot prove that it does not come from denial, delusion or dissociation. All we can say is that Lee is aware of the arguments made by both radical feminist campaigners and conservative Christians – the point here being that the arguments made by those two groups are often strikingly similar – and that Lee rejects them. "A porn performer is always assumed female", Lee notes:

> and it's always assumed to be coercive, or that even if it's her choice, she might have been molested as a child and that's why she decides that she wants to have sex. For someone to believe that a woman has sexual agency – they just can't wrap their mind around it.
>
> (in Tramontana, 2015: np)

Porn as work

When listening to sex workers – that is, when we as researchers treat them as subjects to be listened to and as subjects producing knowledge concerning their occupational practice, rather than as objects to be rescued – we find a very different picture of sex work from that foregrounding objectification and abuse. The claim that sex work is not proper work has been energetically contested by sex work activists in their writing, political campaigning and other forms of organizing (see Chateauvert, 2014; Delacoste, 2018; Smith and Mac, 2018), as well as by researchers studying the conditions and experiences of sex work (see e.g. Kempadoo and Doezema, 1998; Sanders, 2005; Weitzer, 2010). Sex work activists and researchers have argued that, like other forms of labour, this work is diverse in nature; that it involves various degrees of choice, agency and skill; that, like other labourers, sex workers have a range of motivations for doing their work and different experiences of it. Furthermore, sex work should be recognized as "a job not wholly unlike other jobs", and ignoring the diversity of sex workers' experiences and conditions leads to the stigmatization of sex workers as "Other" (Pendleton, 1997: 75), to a material worsening of their work conditions and to increased risks of violence from individuals, the police and the state.

Some activists and writers have emphasized the value of sex work as part of a broader culture of "public sex" (Berlant and Warner, 1998; Califia, 2000) which challenges heteronormative ideals of sex linked to the private sphere, the couple, reproduction and the family. Within the ideology of intimacy that these writers critique, the site of sex is that of committed, monogamous relationships. Casual or anonymous sex, similarly to BDSM, are firmly excluded from the realm of "good sex", as explored in Gayle Rubin's sexual hierarchy (discussed in Chapter 3). The long-term sex worker, artist and campaigner, Annie Sprinkle (1999) for example lists "forty reasons why whores are my heroes" including "Whores challenge sexual mores", "Whores teach people how to be better lovers", "Whores endure in the face of fierce prejudice", "Whores have special talents other people just don't have. Not everyone has what it takes to be a whore" and "Whores are rebelling against the absurd, patriarchal, sex-negative laws against their profession and are fighting for the legal right to receive financial compensation for their valuable work".

Others have emphasized the pleasure taken in the work they do and its importance as part of their identity and self-expression. Feminist and sex-radical sex work has been promoted as a means of "honoring sex and desire" (Queen in Nagle, 1997: 125) while women's involvement in the porn industry has been lauded as "helping shape and change society's views on sexuality" (Milne, 2005: xiii), a tendency that is associated more broadly with the growing visibility of women's perspectives on pornography and other sexually explicit media and with the claim that some forms of pornography may have positive functions as sex education. Indeed, it may be the regulation of pornography that reinforces heteronormative models of sex and obstructs "the emergence of the *kinds* of pornography that have the ability to diversify the genre", thereby marginalizing queer, feminist and kinky sexualities, identities and practices (Stardust, 2014). And, as the example of Lee well illustrates, the people doing porn contribute to knowledge creation concerning the work and products it involves in valuable ways (also Lee and Sullivan, 2016; Taormino et al, 2013).

A view of pornographic labour as progressive has also been evident in accounts of porn as part of a gift economy, produced by amateurs "for the love of it" (see Paasonen, 2010) and freely given. In particular, porn produced by "alternative producers and activist sex workers, younger pro-porn feminists, queer porn networks, aesthetic-technical vanguards, peer-to-peer traders, radical sex/perv cultures, and free-speech activists" (Jacobs, 2007: 3) has been hailed as groundbreaking, working to mix "models of e-commerce as production/consumption alongside intimate personal camaraderie, information sharing, fictional storytelling, and cultural debates" (Jacobs, 2007: 12), blurring boundaries between porn and sexual self-expression more generally. The centralization of amateur online porn distribution on select platforms, alongside the abundance of semi-amateur webcam models, however, challenge any clear detachment of amateur productions from the mainstream of porn. While the field of contemporary online porn is more diverse than ever to date, it also involves a strong pull towards centralized ownership of platforms that sets clear limits to what images and videos are easy to find and who makes money from their distribution (Paasonen, Jarrett and Light, 2019).

At the same time, while it is useful to think about the ways that a gift economy can challenge capitalist conditions of production and consumption, the focus on valuing sex only when it is "for pleasure, not for profit" risks devaluing the labour of those workers who do not do it for free (Ruberg, 2016) and fails to recognize the skills and effort required to perform sex (Smith, 2012). Seeing sex work as valuable only as a site of identity, self-expression and community-building risks marginalizing issues of work and rights; a problem that Alison Phipps (2017) attributes to a continuing dominance of the "sex war" paradigm in feminist inquiry. All the same, as Zahra Stardust argues, it is possible to produce pornography in ways that are valuable in terms of culture and labour, "imagining new lenses through which to see bodies and desires, archiving women's histories, documenting queer sexualities, and focusing on trans* inclusivity and self-deterministic representation" as well as sharing skills and knowledge and advocating for performer access to occupational health and safety and industrial rights, choice over safer sex practices and fair contracts/model releases (Stardust, 2014: 255).

We argue that the refusal by activists and academics to listen to, and to appreciate sex workers' voices, and the insistence that they are passive objects is part of the problem – not part of the solution. "Anti-trafficking" campaigns can be seen as part of a longer history of state interventions focused on public health that have "disproportionately impacted racialized communities, sex workers, and sexually non-normative folks" and that actually operate to marginalize, criminalize or violate the rights of those people (Webber and Sullivan, 2018: 195). In the process, sex workers are presented as a source of contagion and as site of sexually transmitted infection through which the public health crisis of porn may spread, risking to infect the social fabric at large. This involves framing sexual representation through its problematic "effects" or as pointing to the horrors of commercialization of intimate relations more generally. As Heather Berg (2018) argues, both porn performers and fashion models have recently become the site of concern because of the way that consumers will be affected by the objectified images they are involved in coining. Rather than focusing on protecting either set of workers from hostile working conditions, proposals to regulate both pornography and fashion modelling are not really about the health of those working in these industries. Rather, they communicate concerns about how bodies should be presented and looked at, which end up distracting attention from the very real problems that workers face.

How then can we develop ways of understanding sex work that can capture the diversity of that work, value it and remain attentive to conditions of exploitation and inequality? The language of "objectification", we argue, is not the best way to do this. Here, we agree with Danielle Egan (2006: 78) who rejects a radical feminist critique that "abnegates any variation of experience of sex work … denies women who do sex work any type of agency in their decisions to take part in this form of labor" and "marginalizes female sex workers and thus offers little protection or support". Instead, she argues for what she calls *sex radical feminist theory*, which "conceptualizes sexuality and sex work as both deeply embedded in sociocultural inequalities as well as a site of contestation" and allows for a critique of "dominant modes of power and inequality, which often objectify women and are plagued by sexual violence". Rather than calling sex workers "objects", we are better off taking the approach of critical labour scholars who argue that we should understand all work under capitalism to be exploitative (see Weeks, 2011), rather than isolating particular kinds of work such as the sex and beauty industries as bad while letting all other jobs off the hook.

For example, if we compared sex work with academic work, which would be worse for mental health? Higher education staff are, after all, reported to suffer something of an epidemic of mental health issues in all the countries within which the authors of this book work, not making our particular form of office labour particularly "safe". Such an approach would make it possible to see porn labour "as performance, craft … art; and as necessary economic activity" (Lee and Sullivan, 2016: 107). If we "un-exceptionalize" porn as work in this way, as McKee (2016) suggests, we can understand an issue such as condom use in porn production as part of "the larger story of how work impacts on our bodies" (Berg, 2014: 77) and to see where labour practices are similar across industries and where they differ. Importantly, this means respecting the agency of workers to impact the particular forms that their labour takes – as in female porn performers resisting the compulsory use of condoms on set as their use in penetrative sex over several hours is likely to cause abrasions and, hence, result in bodily harm.

Good sex versus BDSM

Jiz Lee is a limit-case study for another reason – they enjoy BDSM which, as mentioned in Chapter 3, has been a contested theme in feminist debates since the 1980s and remains central to debates on sexual objectification. Radical feminist writers have been concerned that BDSM turns women into sexual objects – even if those women are active and enthusiastic participants and seemingly independent of whether they occupy dominant or submissive positions as a dominatrix or a slave.

In her broad critique of pornography and its harmful effects, Robin Morgan, for example, saw it as contributing to "the erosion of the virgin/whore stereotypes to a new 'all women are really whores' attitude, thus erasing the last vestige of (even corrupted) respect for women" (Morgan, 1980: 138). She further saw pornography as resulting in husbands and boyfriends pushing women to "perform sexually in ever more objectified and objectifying fashion", while the more mainstream press extolling "the virtues of anal intercourse, 'fist-fucking', and other 'kinky freedoms'". Here the issue of female sexual pleasure taken in something like anal sex is simply off the table. Rather than involving female sexual agency and desire, sexual practices departing from the norm of "good sex" are positioned as objectifying. Consequently, female desires deemed kinky become understandable as detrimental effects of patriarchal ideology, the boundaries of "normal", socially acceptable sexuality being tightly drawn in the process. If women enjoy kinky, rough or anal sex, so the argument runs, they are objectifying themselves.

Similar concerns have also come to underpin less politically articulated discussions and analyses in a range of settings, not least when these are concerned with the impact and effects of pornography. Porn has been presented, not just as a metaphor for violence, but as a template, even an instruction manual for sexual behaviour. The movement of these ideas into the field of social psychology – a development examined in more detail in Chapter 5 – has helped to solidify this position and to anchor it in relation to existing ways of making sense of the role of media in social life. In particular, the notions of "media effects" and "social learning" have been used to describe and illustrate the impact of media imageries in people's understanding of themselves and others. A concern with media effects has also been drawn on to theorize a link between pornography and violence, and to account for the impact of pornography on men's expectations of sex and on the resulting pressure on women to perform the sexual practices and styles that men may have seen in pornography.

The anti-kink tradition in campaigns against pornography and objectification is by now so widespread and common sense that it may not, on first reading, be obvious what a logically convoluted argument this is: that active sexual demands are signs of being a sexual object. This is common in social psychologist content analysis of pornography (McKee, 2015) and owes much to radical feminist articulations of "good sex" as non-penetrative and anti-kink, as examined in Chapter 3. While we return to the uses of sexual script theory and the difficulties involved in measuring objectification in pornographic representation in Chapter 5, we would like to briefly comment upon the problems involved in scholarly approaches to kinky sex in particular. In analyzing "objectifying scripts" in pornography, Niki Fritz and Bryant Paul, for example, argue that some sexual acts are objectifying, while others show "agency". Their list of "indicators of sexual objectification" includes "stripping, cumshots, aggression, genital focus and gaping"; while indicators of "agency" include "self-touch, orgasm and directing and initiating sex" (Fritz and Paul, 2017: 639). Consensual BDSM – kinky sex – is, they argue, always objectifying, independent of its contexts of production:

> In "Switch", a pornographic scene from the series Rough Sex shot by feminist pornography director Tristan Taormino, actress Sasha Grey tells fellow actor Danny Wylde: "You can slap me if I can slap you". It is the start of a dialogue about what they both like and do not like that leads to a scene where Grey is spit on, slapped, and choked. It is a scene that demonstrates sexual objectification of Grey, where her body is used as an object for male pleasure.
>
> (Fritz and Paul, 2017: 639)

It is worth spending a moment considering this quotation: Sasha Grey tells her sexual partner exactly what she wants, asks for it, and she is in control of the interaction. This – argue Fritz and Paul – is evidence of her objectification. It is not, for them, evidence of agency, or control, or sexual assertiveness. All this is clearly an issue of methodological applications and their premises.

Content analyses of pornography have been concerned to count the amount of "violence" or "aggression" against women in pornography. Despite the taken-for-granted categorizations used in content analyses, the findings produced vary dramatically. Estimates of the amount of aggression in pornography varies between 1.9 percent and 88.8 percent of pornographic material, depending on the study (McKee, 2015: 81). The variation occurs partly because of the wide range of media, historical periods and contexts that are examined in such studies – a fact that suggests that what is being counted as pornographic itself is remarkably varied. As Fritz and Paul show in their own study, comparisons of different types of pornography bear out this variation – mainstream pornography contains significantly more depictions of female objectification than both feminist and for women content, and queer feminist pornography contains significantly more indicators of female sexual agency than both for women and mainstream categories.

But another reason for the variation is the definitions that researchers use to generate their codes of measurement. For example, this widely used definition of violence, "any form of behavior by an individual that intentionally threatens to or does cause physical, sexual or psychological harm to others or themselves" (Stanko, 2001: 316) ignores the issue of consent, and hence the overall context within which images may have been produced, simply counting types of acts that are assumed to meet the definition as "violent". In other definitions, consensual acts are excluded from the category of violence, which comes to signify "Any form of behavior directed toward the goal of harming or injuring another living being who is motivated to avoid such treatment" (Baron and Richardson, 1994: 37). This latter definition operates quite differently in foregrounding not the type of act but its context – whether a person desires the activity or not – as criteria for violence.

Content analyses – the methodological reverberations of which we address further in Chapter 5 – have nevertheless tended to favour the first kind of definition of violence in pornography. Consensual sadomasochism has consequently been recurrently categorized as aggression (see e.g. Malamuth and Spinner, 1980; Scott and Cuvelier, 1993), while any instances of "hair-pulling, hitting, slapping or kicking" have been coded as aggressive (Monk-Turner and Purcell, 1999; see McKee, 2015 for a discussion). Shor and Golriz

(2019) show how these definitions impact on findings in their own study by firstly counting acts that have previously been considered as aggressive and secondly coding whether these were presented as consensual or non-consensual. Using the first definition they found that a total of 43 percent of the videos in their sample included visible physical aggression. Following the second definition, 15.1 percent (sixteen videos) appeared to show non-consensual acts.

In their analysis of aggression in pornographic videos, Ana Bridges et al (2010: 1079) write that we should not "emphasize consent" in looking at violence in pornography, but rather provide a list of "positive sex acts" that include "kissing, hugging and/or giving one another compliments" (Bridges et al, 2010: 1072), acts which Bridges et al understand are positive whether or not they occur with consent. By contrast, they list acts of "aggression" which they argue are negative whether or not they occur with consent – including biting, pinching, pulling hair, spanking, choking, and name calling (Bridges et al, 2010: 1072).

Under this approach, any woman who wants to spank or be spanked, to pull hair or have their hair pulled, choke or be choked will always be a sex object. This isn't a matter of semantics. There is plenty of evidence that kinky sex is completely mainstream in women's sexual fantasies – going back way before the *Fifty Shades of Grey* phenomenon (see discussions in Friday, 1981; Friday, 1993; Friday, 2009). Indeed, Kath Albury (2002) argues that under patri-archy, sexual games of domination and submission are built into the very structure of female sexual imaginaries. This can be understood in two drastically different ways: that, as Albury argues, sexual fantasies in Western cultures come inbuilt with gendered relations of power that fantasies then make it possible to examine and play with, or (in more radical feminist vein) that women are doomed always to be sexual objects until they stop indulging the practices that give them sexual pleasure.

Framing acts such as double penetration as problematic because they are "non-normative" – as that widely quoted study by Bridges et al (2010) does – involves conservative and narrowly hetero-normative ideas of what counts as healthy sexual behaviour. These kinds of views of "unhealthy" sex are less connected to actual harm done to bodies – such practices can be safe – than to moralistic view of "good sex" and its opposites. Descriptors such as "extreme" are applied in varied and disconnected ways – for some authors, scenes of oral sex or casual (non-monogamous) sex are objectifying and degrading simply by virtue of being non-normative. We strongly disagree with this position. Simply counting acts that *seem* aggressive means lumping together practices in ways that ignore their context and the ways they are experienced. Just as in contact sports – from football to ice-hockey or boxing – consensual BDSM may involve activities that appear violent to observers but which are understood very differently by participants.

Is it possible to make a genuine choice to take part in rough sex? What if a woman wants to spank someone, or to be spanked? To have their hair pulled, or to pull someone's hair? To fist someone, to be double-penetrated, to have sex in public, tie someone down, be prodded with needles? Can that be a form of sexual subjectivity? If we measure sexual subjectivity by whether a woman can say "I would not hesitate to ask for what I want sexually from a romantic partner", "I am able to ask a partner to provide the sexual stimulation I need" or "If I were to have sex with someone, I'd show my partner what I want" (Horne and Zimmer-Gembeck, 2006: 132) – all criteria for defining sexual subjectivity discussed in Chapter 5 – then knowing that you enjoy being tied up, or shocked with electrodes, and telling your partner clearly that this is what you want, counts as sexual subjectivity.

But there is another way of deciding what counts as sexual agency – and that is whether or not women make the *right* choices about what they should ask for sexually. This may sound counter-intuitive, but it is a common approach in both radical feminist and psychological writing about pornography – one that is ultimately steeped in moral judgements over the kind of sex that people should engage in, how, why and with whom. In Chapter 5, we move further into the challenges involved in measuring (and hence verifying instances of) objectification in cultural representations and social relations – and hence the fundamental opacity involved in the uses of the concept to start with.

5   Measuring objectification

The methodological question of measuring – and hence providing empirical evidence on – objectification is a difficult one. It remains so even in the context where evidence thereof might seem to be in most ample supply, namely that of mainstream heterosexual pornography, identified by many authors and activists as the quintessential example, or even condensation, of the objectification of women. Building on the discussion on the difficulties involved in identifying sexual violence in pornographic representation, this chapter is concerned with how objectification and sexualization can be or have been measured, what methodological choices this research – or, better, the different research traditions involved – have deployed and what the overall stakes of the debate are. In doing so, we pave way for a discussion on diagnoses on the sexualization and pornification of culture forthcoming in Chapter 6.

Objectification and social psychology

Psychology (along with economics) is one of the most commonly cited academic disciplines in public debate. It is rare for journalists or politicians to quote what a literary theorist has written; it is common for psychologists to be cited. This is partly because while some humanities disciplines always seek out more complexity, social psychology seeks reliable, measurable effects and simple causality, often presenting its findings using language and with a certainty that assures it a significant presence in public debates – it is an "ology", claiming status for itself as a science. When asked about the effects of pornography, a media studies theorist might say

"It's not that simple", while a social psychologist might well say "It's very simple". As Roger Ingham puts this:

> One of the reasons why policy-makers ask psychologists (as opposed to humanities researchers) to work towards developing policy might be because they know that they will get some suggestions – even if they are way off beam and/or just plain wrong; their audience probably won't know they are wrong. On the other hand, asking 50 humanities researchers and getting back 51 answers will not help the policy-makers to sleep at night.
>
> (Ingham, in McKee and Ingham, 2018: 39)

And it is also true that psychology fits well into wider public debates because it tends to align with broader, common sense public discourses rather than (as is the case in some other academic disciplines) challenge them. Social psychological research about pornography has taken two broad approaches. In the first, content analysis seeks to prove that pornography objectifies women as representations. In the second approach, studies of media effects want to show that consuming pornography leads men to objectify women in real life. Content analysis is a form of quantitative textual analysis. Unlike film studies or literary studies which typically use words to describe what happens in a text, content analysis uses numbers, setting out a list of categories to be counted, and then counting then. The aim is to be as "replicable" as possible – this means that if different researchers are given the same text, and the same list of things to count in a film, they will produce the same results. In content analysis of pornography there has been an interest in counting how often women are objectified.

This approach draws on the traditions that we have discussed in the previous chapters – the idea that the most interesting thing about pornography is whether it objectifies people, and the assumption that it is women rather than men who will be objectified, is the result of evolving public debates drawing on the work of radical feminists and film theorists. However, the question of how to "operationalize" the idea of objectification – how to actually count it – reveals some of the difficulties with the term. The concept has been used in public debates in a variety of vague ways: but in order to make it work in content analyses for social psychology you have to decide what you are going to count. All this involves the risk of circular reasoning.

As well as trying to prove that pornography produces objectifying representations of women, social psychology has also sought evidence that consuming pornography makes men more likely to objectify women in real life. Both surveys and experimental studies where sexually explicit material is shown to subjects and their behaviour or attitudes tested have been used extensively to search for pornography's effects. The overall aim of these studies has been to find evidence of pornography's impact on attitudes and behaviours. These researchers have tried to prove that consuming pornography makes men more sexually violent towards women – which is taken to be (as for radical feminism) the ultimate example of "objectification".

As we have discussed in the previous chapters, feminist approaches to pornography have built on the notion of the male gaze and the overall visibility of female bodies, and combined these with other ways of understanding media – particularly the concept of stereotypes and their impact and the idea that media "content" has particular and measurable meanings. Gradually, all of these ideas have been pulled together with psychological and social concepts of sexual scripts and social learning to produce an account of the relation between pornography, power and gender relations. At its simplest, this claims that pornography teaches men how to view women: "men learn to sexualise inequality and objectify women's bodies" (Russo, 1998: 19), and it acts as a means of "legitimizing the objectification of women, and by training men and boys to desire and expect compliant sexual servicing from women and girls" (Whisnant & Stark, 2004: xiv).

Sexual script theory was first outlined in the 1970s by John S. Simon and William Gagnon to account for how the sexual self comes about in webs of internalized and improvised cultural norms. For Simon and Gagnon (1986: 98–9), sexual scripts occur on three levels: as cultural scenarios according to which individuals come to occupy and perform certain roles; as interpersonal scripts emerging in social interactions; and as intrapsychic scripts where personal fantasies and desires meet social meanings. Despite the flexibility afforded by sexual script theory in accounting for how cultural images affect personal desires and actions and how they are adopted and lived with, the model is often applied as a simplified, flattened version where scripts are simply seen as locking people into particular roles, and where porn is seen as a particularly compelling, harmful influence with the power to organize interpersonal and intrapsychic scripts alike. Here, pornography is often depicted as something of a hegemonic sexual script.

Despite some claims to the contrary (Foubert et al, 2011), the results of hundreds of research projects attempting to prove that consuming pornography makes men objectify women have been ambiguous and contradictory. There is no basis in the existing literature to claim that consuming pornography makes men more violent towards women, or to objectify them in other ways (Kohut et al, 2016). It isn't surprising that this is the case, as there are numerous problems with the approach used in these studies.

To start with, in adopting such a narrow focus – the hunt for a link between pornography and violence or objectification – all kinds of other questions and issues are shut down (see McKee et al, 2008: 74–97). As is the case with any investigation into media effects, it is challenging to isolate one element as being the cause of attitudes and behaviours. This "hypodermic needle" model of media effects, highly influential in post-war mass communication research (MCR), where harmful media content has been seen to affect people like a needle filled with venomous substance – be it a vaccination with positive outcomes or a toxin resulting in harm – has been broadly critiqued for its simplified perception of media reception as involving top–down effects. In studies of pornography's effects, this model isolates pornography (as a causative element) from the broader social and cultural fabric. Studies seeking to identify the impact of porn on men's attitudes towards women or sexual violence, for example, do not account for the role of attitudes that the people studied have grown up with in families, schools, churches or other social settings, or their broader patterns of media consumption. If, following Teresa de Lauretis (1987), media operate as "technologies of gender" that produce ways of understanding and doing gender, the same also applies to the school, the state and the church. Pornography can be one social technology of gender but it is not the only one, nor does it operate in uniform ways.

Since they aim to isolate and show proof of stimulus and effect, experimental studies are completely artificial. They work with subjects who may or may not be consumers of pornography, placing them in settings which are nothing like those in which pornography would usually be watched and showing them pornography that they have not chosen to watch. The setting, in sum, is far detached from how pornography is ordinarily consumed: in private spaces, out of one's own volition and with materials of one's own preference and choosing. In some studies, the bodily reactions of study participants are monitored and measured in laboratory settings, further adding to the artificiality of the enterprise. In others, evidence is collected through self-reporting or surveys charting opinions and attitudes, possibly both before and after the research subjects have been "exposed" to pornographic materials (see e.g. Kingston and Malamuth, 2011).

Crucially, surveys often confuse *causation* (an effect – for example, the idea that consuming pornography causes people to become more sexually adventurous) with *correlation* (two factors that happen at the same time and may be related but which do not demonstrate an effect). For example, if we find that people who consume pornography may also be more sexually adventurous, we can report that as saying that sexually adventurous people are more likely to watch pornography; or that people who watch pornography are more likely to be sexually adventurous. Similarly, should we say that men who are convicted of rape are more likely to watch violent pornography; or that people who watch violent pornography are more likely to be convicted of rape? Often, studies in this tradition suggest they have found effects, or causations, even though their own data do not demonstrate this. For example, Braun-Courville and Rojas state that they were "unable to establish whether exposure to sexually explicit material leads to engagement in sexual behavior or whether those individuals who partake in more high-risk sexual behaviors also have a tendency to seek out sexually explicit Web sites" (Braun-Courville and Rojas, 2009: 161). Yet they also use their study to claim that "prolonged exposure to pornography can lead to sexually permissive attitudes" (Braun-Courville and Rojas, 2009: 157).

Lastly, these kinds of studies are often built on a conservative view of sex and gender, for example, seeing casual sex or active female sexuality as problems or risks. For example, Peter and Valkenburg's 2007 study claimed to find a relationship between exposure to sexually explicit material and "beliefs that women are sex objects" (Peter and Valkenburg, 2007: 381). But on closer examination, one of the measures of "objectification" was whether people agreed with the statement "Sexually active girls are more attractive partners" (Peter and Valkenburg, 2007: 389). There is nothing necessarily objectifying in this statement.

Ambivalent outcomes

In his study on objectification in Australian mainstream video porn, Alan McKee (2005), building on the tradition of close textual analysis in film studies, proposes twelve measures for analyzing objectification. The first measures concern reciprocity: (1) who initiates sex; (2) the number of orgasms different people have in each scene; (3) the kinds of sex acts that are performed; and (4) the kinds of sex acts that are causing orgasms. The next five address identification with characters as subjects: (5) who the central characters are; (6) which characters are named; (7) the time that different characters spend talking to one other; (8) the time they spend looking at the camera; and (9) the time they spend speaking to the camera. For measuring instances of violence, the categories are: (10) the number of scenes including non-consensual physical sexual violence; (11) the number of scenes including non-consensual use of sexually violent language; and (12) the number of scenes including other forms of non-consensual sex. These measures were then applied to coding 838 scenes in the fifty best-selling Australian porn films.

According to the findings, female characters initiated sex more often than male ones, yet had fewer orgasms. Sexual acts were varied, there was no gender disparity in who the central characters were, in whether they had names, or how much time they spent speaking to other characters. Women however "returned the gaze" by looking directly at the camera more often than men, and also spent more time talking at it: according to some measures, then, male characters were objectified more than female ones; and according to other measures, female characters were more objectified.

The study speaks to the difficulty of measuring objectification, as well as what is basically the hypocrisy of some previous research in the area. For example, in heterosexual porn, it is not unusual for male characters to be depicted primarily through their genitalia: their heads can be framed off and attention seldom lingers on their facial expressions or other personal characteristics. However, this is not usually taken to mean that men are rendered powerless by being objectified in pornography as faceless cocks and fuck machines valued especially for their ability to ejaculate on cue. Female bodies are often differently positioned so that it is not only the body but also the face that is being displayed. And yet it is rare to hear activists arguing that this means that women are less objectified in pornography. It sometimes appears to be the case that pornography researchers have already decided what they are to discover before launching their inquiries. Informed by public debates and activism, they act as if they already know, before they start gathering data, that pornography objectifies women. Data is then gathered and analyzed in ways that support this pre-existing commitment. It is rare that content analyses compare the objectification of men with women; it is rather assumed as a starting point that women will be more objectified, and the studies set out to measure how this happens.

It is worth making explicit that we are not saying that pornography is not sexist. It is often incredibly sexist. But that is separate from porn being sexually explicit. One can be sexually explicit without being sexist. And one can be sexist without being sexually explicit. Pornography is a part of a sexist culture – but that does not provide evidence for porn being the root cause of sexism in culture. In focusing on porn as the theory of, or recipe for, violence against women, anti-pornography feminism positions sexually explicit imagery as a damaging force impacting culture. If, however, we understand pornography as a field of cultural production rather than a nefarious effect invading society and culture as if from the outside, it is obvious that porn can be sexist and racist since culture comes with sexist and racist biases and practices. This does not mean that *all* pornography is sexist and racist, given the range and diversity of sexually explicit representations.

Addictive, risky pornographic objects

A more extreme version of views connected to the harmful impact of porn has emerged in the more recent idea of it being addictive in the same way as a drug, operating materially on the brain by flooding it with pleasure chemicals, building a dependency and rewiring the brain. Anti-addiction websites encourage people to diagnose themselves through self-administered online tests and growing numbers of therapists offer treatment for porn addiction. These frequently characterize addiction as a process of dehumanization in which artificial stimuli such as pornography attack the natural functioning of the human brain, harming male consumers of pornography in particular. This rhetoric then makes it possible to foreground men as the true victims of porn – a stance adopted in the broadly visible, Reddit-based NoFap movement, the supporters of which have been known for vitriolically attacking female scholars not sharing their view on the harms caused by masturbation.

This approach is, then, obviously linked to long-standing worries about objectification. Its view of sexuality draws on an idea of solo sex, the autoerotic, and in particular male masturbation, as inauthentic (Tuck, 2009). Concerns about men's compulsive masturbation – or "self-pollution" were commonplace in eighteenth, nineteenth and early twentieth century medical literature, seen as a withdrawal from the social world (Laqueur, 2003). The more recent panic about porn addiction draws heavily on this view, with porn isolating men from human contact and from their natural sexuality, to the extent that it produces erectile dysfunction and the inability to have or enjoy "real", that is, penetrative heterosexual sex with a human partner. Commentators worry that men are literally only able to have sexual relations with objects – pornographic images – and not with other human beings.

A particularly narrow view of "healthy sex" underpins this and the variety of concerns with sexual wellbeing or "slow sex" where, for example, sexual energy is understood as a natural force which can become "poorly channelled" due to a "society that constantly bombards us with images of sex that have very little to do with healthy sexuality" – a formulation repeated verbatim in numerous sexual health and counselling sites. For example, both Gail Dines and Wendy Malz use the term "porn sex", which involves using someone, separates sex from love, is about gratifying impulses and compromising values, and turns sex into a performance and commodity. In contrast "healthy sex" is about "caring for someone" and "sharing with a partner", a "private experience", "an expression of love" and "nurturing" that "involves all the senses", "enhances who you really are", and provides "lasting satisfaction". Dines claims that porn "renders all authentic desire plastic. The images, messages and stories of pornography have seeped into and distorted our genuine sexual identities" (Dines, 2011). Here sex has become "industrialized" (see Dines, 2011; Jeffreys, 2008) in contrast to the authentic sex that "develops organically out of life experiences, one's peer group, personality traits, family and community affiliations" (Dines, 2011: xi). Discourses of porn addiction draw on this view of porn, with some sites such as Your Brain on Porn recommending a process of "rebooting" which suggests that natural and healthy sexuality can be restored through abstinence from "artificial sexual stimulation". Once again, objectification is a threat – for these activists, if sex does not involve love then it is objectifying.

"Fight the New Drug", a Utah-based anti-pornography NGO founded in 2009 targets young adults in particular through social media, and loosely basing its argument on neuroscientific rhetoric according to which online porn, in its abundantly available and diverse forms, is an addictive toxic substance that needs to be countered with yet another "war on drugs". This argument is supported by activist groups identifying pornography as a "public health crisis" that is also currently adopted in a dozen or so US states at the level of policy. According to this concern, porn makes men unable to have sex with women, preferring pornographic representational and masturbatory practices instead. In a further expansion of this concern, sex dolls, as pornographic stand-ins for women, are making sexual relations even more strained and dangerous for women.

During the time of writing this book, the emergence of sex robot brothels in various parts of the world, from Toronto to London, Barcelona, Paris and Helsinki, mainly populated by dolls with female gender characteristics, has resulted in public concerns about the objectification and dehumanization of women. Writing for *The Feminist Current*, the radical feminist author Meghan Murphy (2017) identifies sex robots as symbols of patriarchy – a system of male government and power – epitomizing the objectification of women. For their part, the activists of Fight the New Drug (2018), see robot brothels as involving "the literal objectification and perpetuation of gender inequalities". Meanwhile, three Swedish feminist groups (Sveriges Kvionnolobby, Roks and Unizon) have jointly called for legal action over sex robots that reproduce the "objectified, sexualized, and degraded woman found in contemporary mainstream pornography", and which they see as contributing to rape culture, pedophilia, and the dehumanization of women, and justifying sexual exploitation and slavery (Berglund et al, 2019).

These commentators position sex robots as interactive sex toys bearing human characteristics, as products of patriarchy that both symbolize and further support the objectification and dehumanization of women, as well as fuel sexual violence against them. The heart of the debate here concerns the interrelations between sex, objects and people, as well as the slippage between life-like objects such as sex dolls and human women being reduced to sexual objects. Jennifer S. Saul (2006: 58–9) has discussed a similar dynamic as one of personification – "using an object to fulfill the function of a person" – and the corresponding objectification as treating a person as a mere means to an end.

According to critiques of sex robots, they contribute to an understanding of women as disposable, instrumental objects of male heterosexual gratification, hence speaking of a patriarchal more than a capitalist ideology. Following this line of thinking, human-like sex dolls render the objectified status of women literal by replacing the woman with an object void of agency – in a vein possibly reminiscent of the dystopian 1975 sci-fi film, *The Stepford Wives*, where men replace their wives with machine replicas focused on housework and sexual servitude. The slippage between female bodies and robot dolls representing women, while involving a considerable leap, seems to be both quick and easy. This, of course, is in line with the radical feminist critiques examined throughout this book, according to which "when object-hood is projected onto women, women not only seem more object-like, but are made to become more object-like" (Langton, 2009: 12) – a development which pornography in particular is seen to fuel and accelerate.

If, say, a person wants to have sex with a robot doll marked as female, this would, according to this line of thinking, imply that the person is willing, or even likely to treat actual human women as similar objects of pleasure, should he be able to, or that he would at least wish for women to occupy such an instrumental role. That a person might want to have sex with a robot precisely for the very virtue of the object being a doll and not a living person is an option more seldom discussed (see De Fren 2008; 2009a; 2009b), as is the possibility that people may move between having different kinds of sex with both dolls and people without conflating the human and the nonhuman, the animate and the inanimate, or establishing similar bonds and sexual dynamics with them.

At first glance, the conflation of sex robots and women as sexual objects may make sense – these dolls being, after all, stylized after the female body. Looked at more closely, this conflation, performed as feminist critique, assumes similarity between ontologically different bodies – ones of flesh, mucus, fat and bone with affective, cognitive and somatic capacities, and those of silicone, plastic and steel performing pre-programmed actions – assuming that the ways of treating the latter not only reflect, but will also damagingly affect the treatment of the former. This negative impact is premised on the model of media effects, within which pornography forms the template for the objectification of women that is then fully carried out in engagements with sex robots, and which threatens to impact sexual relations between people, as well. Ultimately, this easy conflation of dolls and women speaks of how pervasive, even commonsensical, the vocabulary of objectification has become in public discourse, as well as the rhetorical power that it holds despite the practical difficulties involved in measuring or even defining its forms and effects in empirical inquiry.

The example of technologically advanced sex dolls and the cultural debates connected to them makes evident the necessity of asking what qualifies, or is meant by sex as such and how these understandings become mapped onto social and moral norms concerning appropriate demeanour. The spectre of "good sex" never looms too far away in how judgements are made over people's masturbation habits connected to porn or to sex toys of different kinds – of which sex robots are, quintessentially, one variation. The easy conflation of dolls and women assumes similarity, or at least continuity in how they are treated, what kinds of agency they may have and what kinds of heterosexual dynamics they operate (or are operated) in.

Objectification and/as sexualization

If pornography is seen to causally make men objectify women, then what makes women buy into the overall logic of fashioning themselves as objects of the male gaze? Feminist critiques of pornography mostly ignore the female consumers of the genre, implying that pornography is a technology of gender impacting the behaviour of men but not that of women – or at least not directly, through women engaging with such imageries. In the final part of this chapter, we look at social psychology research on objectification as a concern about women's relationships with their own bodies. This brings us to the fundamental question of how objectification and sexualization have been brought together and, to a degree, conflated with one another.

Research in social psychology has drawn strongly on the language of objectification that has developed from radical feminism and film studies, and – in turn – this psychological research feeds into public debates about sexual representation and objectification. All this has fed into public discourse and, consequently, into ways of understanding the impact of media. Writing for young women's lifestyle magazine *Bustle*, Suzannah Weiss (2017) identified "objectification" with the harmful pressure of beauty norms. In her account of the harms of objectification, Weiss drew largely on the *Report of the American Psychological Association Task Force on the Sexualization of Girls* (Zurbriggen et al, 2010) – collapsing objectification and sexualization together as though they were the same thing. Disordered eating, difficulty in school, depression, neglect of inner beauty, and relationship problems for men are identified as "5 Negative effects of objectifying women, according to science". In other words, the objectification of women results in stressful and limiting body norms, unhappiness, skewed social expectations and relations, effectively eating away at the quality of life.

During the 1990s, social psychologists began to take the arguments of feminist activists and philosophers about women's appearance and bodies under patriarchy and translate them into the supposedly neutral language, quantitative scales and measurements of social science. When previous social psychologists had been concerned about how women thought about their bodies, their approaches had not been "based on feminist theory" (McKinley and

Hyde, 1996: 182). In contrast, this new generation of researchers explicitly set out to translate feminist concerns into the language of social psychology, and thus to reframe feminist body politics as *scholarly*.

The work of Nita McKinley and Janet Hyde in particular represents an important and much-cited starting point for social scientific research on the ways in which women see themselves as objects of someone else's gaze. McKinley and Hyde explicitly set out to translate knowledge from feminist writers in order to "measure the behaviors and attitudes [that] contribute to women's negative body experience" (McKinley and Hyde, 1996: 182). McKinley (in earlier work that forms the basis of the article) drew on journalist Naomi Wolf's widely read and internationally translated *The Beauty Myth* (Wolf, 1991), communication researcher Carole Spitzack's *Confessing Excess: women and the politics of body reduction* (Spitzack, 1990) and philosopher Sandra Bartky's (1988) work on Foucault and feminism to develop her theory of OBC – Objectified Body Consciousness (McKinley and Hyde, 1996: 183) – the degree to which women think of themselves, and value themselves, as objects to be looked at. They argue that "[h]igher levels of OBC are theorized to lead to negative body experience for women" (McKinley and Hyde, 1996: 183).

In order to turn philosophy and journalism into social psychology, McKinley and Hyde sought to develop valid and quantifiable variables, discovering three valid variables relevant to identifying OBC. The first is "body surveillance" – the degree to which women are "seeing themselves as others see them" (McKinley and Hyde, 1996: 183) and measured using the "Surveillance scale" survey instrument that included questions such as "I rarely compare how I look with how other people look" and "I am more concerned with what my body can do than how it looks" (McKinley and Hyde, 1996: 191). The second variable – "internalization of cultural standards and body shame" (McKinley and Hyde, 1996: 183) – was measured via questions such as "When I can't control my weight, I feel like something must be wrong with me" and "I would be ashamed for people to know what I really weigh" (McKinley and Hyde, 1996: 191). The degree to which a woman believes she ultimately has control over how she looks, "Control beliefs", was the third variable identified by McKinley and Hyde (1996: 184), measured using questions such as "I think a person can look pretty much how they want to if they are willing to work at it" and "I can weigh what I'm supposed to when I try hard enough" (McKinley and Hyde, 1996: 192–3).

It will be apparent that – although there are some questions that are more generally about whether they "look pretty" – the key focus of these scales is women's relationship with their weight. When the authors are concerned that "cultural standards for the feminine body are virtually impossible to realize fully" (McKinley and Hyde, 1996: 184) they are primarily addressing dieting – or, as they call it, in a term that is both scientifically neutral and simultaneously feminist – "restricted eating" (McKinley and Hyde, 1996: 181). The authors then demonstrate that women who are strongly concerned with their weight, feel shame if their body does not reach the cultural ideal of slenderness, and believe that it is their own fault if they do not match the cultural ideal of beauty, are more likely to have a problematic relationship with food, eating and their own bodies. All this makes sense.

It is important to note that this research in fact says nothing about "sexualization": a woman can be curvy or skinny and either present herself as sexy or as not sexy, as the two variables are not related. McKinley and Hyde do not use the word "sexualization" in their work. When they are reporting about women who suffer from body shame and who diet, there is no sense that this is related to how "sexy" those women are, or perceive themselves as being. At this point the concern is only "objectification".

McKinley and Hyde's work was important in beginning to establish the language of "objectification theory" in social psychology. It is the work of two other researchers, Barbara L. Fredrickson and Tomi-Ann Roberts, published in the following year, that provides the most commonly-cited theoretical framework for objectification (Fredrickson and Roberts, 1997) – indeed, the most-cited article published by the journal *Psychology of Women Quarterly* (Fredrickson et al, 2011: 689). Fredrickson and Roberts' essay is similar to McKinley and Hyde's in that it explicitly presents itself as taking the language of feminist theory and bringing it into social psychology. In this, their essay is a magisterial work of translation, drawing on a wide and important range of writing by feminist philosophers from the radical feminist author and poet Adrienne Rich to the psychoanalyst and author of *Fat Is a Feminist Issue* (1978), Susie Orbach – and translating it into the formal language of the social sciences.

However, there are also important differences between this article and the earlier work, as Fredrickson and Roberts present an "Objectification theory" that is *only* concerned about the ways that culture sexually objectifies women (Fredrickson and Roberts, 1997: 173). This work then represents the shift in social psychology that starts to argue that objectification is the same thing as sexualization. From this point onwards, social psychology – and the public debates that draw on this research – began to collapse these two issues together.

Moreover, while the earlier writers present a focused and measurable approach to objectification – women who feel shame that their body does not match the cultural ideal are more likely to have a problematic relationship with food – Fredrickson and Roberts's theory is more generalized. They are not testing particular variables or offering a particular survey instrument. Rather, they are proposing an overarching theory of some of the relationships that might exist between women's "objectification" and various negative mental health outcomes, including eating disorders, sexual dysfunction, and depression (Fredrickson and Roberts, 1997: 186, 189, 190). They do not specify that they are talking about women's shame if their body does not match the cultural ideal, but talk more broadly about women's concern with their "physical appearance" (Fredrickson and Roberts, 1997: 177). As Fredrickson argues in a later co-authored article:

> Objectification theory suggests the consequences of self-objectification occur solely as a result of being concerned with physical appearance, regardless of individuals' level of satisfaction with their physical appearance. That is, women who are satisfied with their bodies as well as those who are dissatisfied with their bodies may each experience the negative consequences of self-objectification simply because they are concerned with their appearance.
>
> (Noll and Fredrickson, 1998: 629)

This is an important difference. The earlier writers argue that *body shame* has negative effects on mental health, while Fredrickson and Roberts in fact argue that *any concern* with appearance has negative effects. Even this is not the whole story, however. One can be concerned with one's appearance without wanting to be overtly sexy (as every female politician has to be, for example). Fredrickson and Roberts (1997: 198) are not, however, particularly concerned about women who are preoccupied with their appearance in an appropriate, nice, middle-class way. Rather, their primary concern is with women who wear high heeled shoes, tight clothing, shave their legs and wear makeup. In other words, for them, it is women who want to appear sexy in accordance with mainstream codes of femininity who are the problem. While the "No More Miss America" activists threw the symbols of commercial femininity into the freedom trashcan, women objectifying themselves readily embrace these – the objects of feminist critique remaining near-identical.

For example, the "Trait self-objectification questionnaire" developed by Noll and Fredrickson (reproduced in Fredrickson and Harrison, 2005: 96–7) asks women "When considering your physical self-concept, how important is ..." followed by a list of characteristics including "physical coordination", "strength", "energy level" and "sex appeal". Using this scale, Fredrickson and Harrison are concerned to note that women who rate their physical coordination and energy level higher than their sex appeal are better at sporting activities, such as throwing, than women who rate their appearance as more important that their sporting prowess. They summarize this to indicate that "hyperconcern for appearance ... predicts diminished motor performance" (Fredrickson and Harrison, 2005: 92).

On this point, we make two responses. The first is to remind readers that to "predict" in the language of statistics does not mean what it means in everyday life. It does not mean "allows us to make a hypothesis about future events". In statistics to say that one variable "predicts" another merely means that they are correlated – i.e. women who are not so good at sport are likely to also care more about their appearance, and vice versa. Our second response – as a group of authors who were not good at sport at school, particularly the two queer men in the writing team – is that we do not see sporting prowess as a necessary part of a healthy life for everyone. A model that demands "sports participation" as evidence of a woman's healthy relationship to her body (Fredrickson and Roberts, 1997: 198) is fine for those who like such things, but fills these authors, still carrying the psychological scars from school PE many decades ago, with dread.

Importantly, in the work of Fredrickson and Roberts (and also in the earlier work of McKinley) there is little possibility of difference or agency on the part of women. In their consistent use of the language of "internalized" objectification there is a dismissal of women's consent in a patriarchal culture. McKinley and Hyde write that:

> Internalization of cultural body standards makes it appear as though these standards come from within the individual woman and makes the achievement of these standards appear to be a personal choice rather than a product of social pressure. Women themselves want to be "beautiful".
>
> (McKinley and Hyde, 1996: 183)

Fredrickson and Roberts agree that:

> a critical repercussion of being viewed by others in sexually objectifying ways is that, over time, individuals may be coaxed to internalize an observer's perspective on self, an effect we term self-objectification. Girls and women, according to our analysis, may to some degree come to view themselves as objects or "sights" to be appreciated by others.
>
> (Fredrickson and Roberts 1997: 179–80)

These models of "internalization" do not allow for considerations of women's agency, sexual performance, or instances of and pleasures in female exhibitionism, for example – indeed, these are modes that "objectification theory" does not comment on. All this allows objectification theory a certain simplified clarity through which the conflation of objectification with sexualization, while by no means obvious or straightforward comes to be presented as commonsensical. The effects of this conflation, we argue, are far-reaching and elementary in and for understanding objectification as a concern of feminist activism and research. Having mapped out some of the complexities in how objectification has been understood and measured, in Chapter 6 we move on to the broader implications of the concept in accounting for the sexualization of culture and, consequently, the possibilities of female agency within it.

6 What to do with sexualized culture?

We have noted in the previous chapters that of the huge number of social and cultural issues addressed by second-wave feminism – marriage, parenting, abortion, education and representation across all media genres – pornography has taken a central place in public arguments about objectification. In particular, we have noted that while early second-wave feminism was in fact as concerned with advertising, television, magazines, popular music and films (Bronstein, 2011) as it was with pornography, a certain strand of radical feminism, strategically allied with Conservative Christians and other right-wing groups, focused on pornography as the single most important issue to be addressed, to the exclusion of other media genres.

More recently, we have seen the reintroduction into public debate of feminist concerns about other media genres – writers argue that we should be concerned about the representation of women in genres such as advertising and music videos because these genres are actually *a kind of pornography* and hence both sexist and harmful in contributing to the objectification of women. What is interesting to note is that whereas it would have seemed extraordinary to consider the "ordinary media" of the 1980s and 1990s pornographic – unless you were one of those fantastic "bra-burning feminists" – now contemporary culture has been identified as "pornographicized" (McNair, 2002; McNair, 2013), "pornified" (Gill, 2008; Mulholland, 2013; Paasonen, Nikunen and Saarenmaa, 2007; Paul, 2005), and "porned" (Sarracino and Scott, 2008). Addressing these broader diagnoses of pornified culture, Chapter 7 equally examines the ambiguities involved in telling sexual subjectivity and objectification apart.

In different ways, such diagnoses have set out to account for how the role that pornography, in its diverse sub-genres, plays in everyday lives and how flirtation with the codes of both softcore and hardcore – the sexually suggestive and the sexually explicit – cuts through media culture more widely. In addition, a range of concerns over pornification are being voiced on online platforms, some of which are Christian in origin, others more unclear in their politics, and yet others left-leaning, right-wing, feminist and activist. Pornification is debated by journalists and in the kinds of policy documents identified above, resulting in something of a "cacophony of concern" (Smith, 2010: 103). The idea that culture has been "pornified" links to another key term in debates about objectification, namely that of "sexualization". As discussed in Chapter 5, the notion of sexualization is commonly used in public debates as though it is a synonym for objectified: that to be sexualized is to be an object. This chapter sets out to examine what diagnoses of sexualization and pornification encompass, and what they aim to achieve. How do they profit, or limit, cultural inquiry?

Girls gone skank

The term "sexualization" originally emerged in sociological research in the 1970s to describe "sexual socialization" – "the development of a gender identity; acquisition of sexual skills, knowledge, and values, and of sexual attitudes or disposition to behave" (Spanier, 1975, in Duschinsky, 2013). In its original use, sexualization was a neutral term – understood as a necessary part of healthy human sexual development. We all had to be "sexualised" as part of growing up – that is, we all had to learn how to conduct ourselves as sexual beings according to the rules of the culture in which we were raised. As McKee et al argue in their multidisciplinary framework for healthy sexual development, it is vital that young people develop an understanding of "parental and societal values" about sex and sexuality (McKee et al, 2010: 17) – even if they choose not to follow those values in their entirety.

The meaning of the term "sexualization" has, however, changed dramatically since. Being "sexualized" is now understood as a negative thing, synonymous with being "objectified". Its use is a way of expressing concern about girls "growing up too quickly", and about a visibility of sex and the accessibility of sexual representations amounting to a "sexualization of culture". That last term appeared in policy reviews and government reports in the United States, Australia and the United Kingdom in the first decade of the twenty-first century (Rush and La Nauze, 2006; American Psychological Association (APA), 2007; Papadopoulos and Home Office, 2010; Bailey and Department for Education, 2011), as well as a variety of well-publicized popular books including Ariel Levy's *Female Chauvinist Pigs: Women and the Rise of Raunch Culture* (Levy, 2005), Carol Platt Liebau's *Prude* (Liebau, 2007), Patrice Oppliger's *Girls gone skank: The sexualization of girls in American culture* (Oppliger, 2008) and Meenakshi Gigi Durham's *The Lolita Effect* (Durham, 2008).

While united in their expressions of concern and the presentation of both sex and the media as problems, these bodies of literature have taken a range of approaches to sexualization – sometimes made very clear, for example in Liebau's concerns about "innocence" and "standards" or the presentation of girls behaving as "skanks" in Oppliger's book. But in more apparently neutral accounts "sexualization" has also been employed in quite diverse ways, even within the same document. In different parts of the Bailey Review (Bailey and Department for Education, 2011), sexualization is used to refer to four very different things – the visibility of sexual content in public; misogyny; children's sexuality; and "deviant" sexual behaviour (see Barker and Duschinsky, 2012). Sexualization also took four forms in the APA Report:

> Sexualization occurs when 1. a person's value comes only from his or her sexual appeal or behavior, to the exclusion of other characteristics; 2. a person is held to a standard that equates physical attractiveness (narrowly defined) with being sexy; 3. a person is sexually objectified – that is, made into a thing for others' sexual use, rather than seen as a person with the capacity for independent action and decision making; 4. sexuality is inappropriately imposed upon a person.
>
> (APA, 2007: np)

As the APA Report notes, most of its discussion refers to the third of these forms – namely sexual objectification. Across this wide range of approaches to "sexualization", one version has vanished – the belief that "sexualization" ("sexual socialization") is a necessary part of healthy sexual development. It has been recast as only ever a negative thing, and one intimately tied in with the dynamics of objectification. This is evident in how various "Sexualisation reports" (APA, 2007; Bailey and Department for Education, 2011; Papadopoulos and Home Office, 2010; Rush and La Nauze, 2006), tend to confuse sexualization with objectification. The authors of the APA report defined "sexualization" as occuring when girls (and only girls) "sexualize themselves when they see themselves mostly or exclusively in sexual terms and when they equate their sexiness with a narrow standard of physical attractiveness", or when they "think of themselves in objectified terms...as objects to be looked at and evaluated for their appearance" (APA, 2007: 17). There is no possibility of healthy sexual socialization in this approach.

Thus these reports offer a particular "frame" for thinking about objectification and sexualization. Such framing performs a function – there are always multiple ways we might research and report on an issue (Tucker, 1998) – including how we approach problem definition, diagnosis, evaluation and policy recommendation. Framing offers a particular way of approaching an issue provides a "common stock of key words, phrases, images, sources, and themes" and highlighting and promotes "specific facts, interpretations and judgments", thereby shaping how an issue is discussed (Tucker, 1998: 143).

In 1995, a Calvin Klein advertising campaign took the form of an audition in which a man, off camera, directed, questioned and complimented a series of young looking male and female models. Lauren R. Tucker (1998) explored how discussions of the campaign fostered concern and controversy by using a "kiddie-porn" frame which presented Klein as a modern-day Fagin exploiting the campaign's models as immature, sexually deviant and low social status victims. Critical statements by institutions such as the American Family Association and the FBI were accompanied by a "Greek chorus of critics" – advertising critics, marketing experts, and fashion industry spokespeople and it was reported that the campaign had caused "public outrage" even though no "ordinary" members of the public were invited to speak (nor were the models themselves). Tucker argues that this frame produced an image of youth as erratic and amoral, along with common-sense beliefs about the nature of youth, youthful sexuality and youthful cultural and economic power.

Similar framing occurs in the reports on sexualization that have become so important to public debates about objectification. Although such reports claim to analyze all of the evidence, they overwhelmingly draw on social psychology research, as discussed in Chapter 5. In doing this, they build on media effects approaches to thinking about media and their consumers – and exclude other research traditions which offer more expansive understandings of the relationships between sex and media, culture and technology, and which have often foregrounded young people's experiences and stories – such as media and cultural studies, critical sociology and psychology, youth and girl studies and much of gender and sexuality studies. An enormous amount of feminist research is also excluded in the process. Reflecting on the Report by Linda Papadopoulos and the Home Office, Lynne Segal noted that it was "as though the last forty years of feminist and other scholarly contention around the body, sexuality and representation, had simply never happened" (Segal, 2010: np).

In the Report by Papadopoulos and the Home Office, the term "sexualization" is used as a way of describing "a number of trends in the production and consumption of contemporary culture" where "the common denominator is the use of sexual attributes as a measure of a person's value and worth" (Papadopoulos and Home Office, 2010: 24), managing to suggest that sexualization is the same as "sexual objectification" (ibid: 27), or "gender stereotypical ideas and images" (ibid: 37). In another passage the report refers to "sexualisation and Objectification" (ibid: 83), as though these were distinct. In other places, it is "premature sexualisation" (ibid: 36) or "hyper-sexualisation" (ibid: 62) that are identified as problems. These varying uses of the term obscure what is under discussion – is it a problematic expression of sexuality at any age or one that has developed too early? Is it the same as objectification or gender stereotyping, distinct from or related to these? Similarly, the Bailey Review lists what it describes as four objects of parental concerns – "early sexualisation", content and practices which are "sexually suggestive", which treat women as "sexual only", which encourage "children to think of themselves (or others to think of children) as adult or sexual", and which are "glamorising or normalising 'deviant' behaviour" (Bailey and Department for Education, 2011: 4).

But these quite different areas of concern are dealt with in ways that show how such reports both ignore public opinion and promote views that are often hostile to girls and women. For example, while the review notes that parents are concerned with both "sexualised and gender-stereotyped clothing, products and services for children" (Bailey and Department for Education, 2011: 15) – not just "sexy" clothing but "pink and blue clothing, ultra-feminine clothes for girls and army or sports clothes for boys" it only recommends that retailers should avoid selling sexualised clothing (ibid: 44), claiming that there is "no strong evidence that gender stereotyping in marketing or products influences children's behaviour" (ibid: 48), and that gender preferences are, in any case, strongly biologically driven and part of the "normal, healthy development of gender identity" (ibid: 49). 13.4 percent of parents reported their concern about sexualized covers of lads' mags, but more than half were concerned about the objectification of women and beauty standards in a range of magazines and newspapers. The report criticizes the "sexually suggestive" content of lads' mags and their promotion of "deviant" practices and recommends removing them from the view of children, but ignores the other publications, along with the issues of airbrushing, thin models and lack of diversity of body forms, which parents complained about. By muddling together parents' concerns about sexualization, objectification and gender stereotyping, the report is able to discount issues of gender inequalities and focus its criticism on sexual deviance and suggestiveness.

Although it is not the central focus of this book, we also note that there are significant academic problems with the ways these reports gather, analyze and report on their evidence. They are highly selective in the kinds of evidence they use and not clear or consistent about the authority and credibility of these. For example, in its section on "Lap-dancing and glamour modelling", the Report by Papadopoulos and the Home Office draws on evidence from three academic writers (Phil Hubbard, Danielle Egan and Rosalind Gill), a Home Office report, a parliamentary paper, a *Times* news report (Deeley, 2008) and an OBJECT! campaign. The news report is used as the source for a claim that "63% of young women would rather be glamour models than nurses, doctors or teachers"; a statistic that comes from an online survey carried out for a mobile entertainment company that asked 1,000 girls aged fifteen to nineteen whether they'd rather be like "Abi Titmuss, Germaine Greer or Anita Roddick" (a glamour model, a feminist writer and an entrepreneur and environmental campaigner), with 63 percent picking Titmuss. There are problems with generalizing from that survey – after all, both Germaine Greer and Anita Roddick are controversial figures for young feminists as much as anybody else – and it is not clear that the survey was ever even undertaken, but nevertheless the statistic was repeated widely including in OBJECT!'s FAQ on lads' mags (2005), the NUS Women's Campaign Policy (2009), and Kat Banyard's book *The Equality Illusion* (2011) (see Ditum, 2012).

Too often, these reports make complex issues appear simple, "obvious" and easy to understand. They collapse a range of issues together, thereby allowing commentators to "slip from one to the other as though any of them were saying the same thing, with any of them either being a cause or an effect" (McKee, 2010: 131–4). While important concerns are aired, their discussions work to obscure rather than illuminate the specifics of the concerns (Smith, 2010; McKee, 2010; Egan, 2013; Evans and Riley, 2015). In the process, sexualization becomes "a disorienting context in which to think about contemporary gender relations" (Evans and Riley, 2015), a distraction from discussion and a substitute for action.

Acting sexy

As noted above, the "media effects" model remains influential in studies of media and objectification. Rebecca Coleman (2008: 164) points out that media effect research tends to identify the effects of media on its consumers as both linear and victimizing, in that representations propagating narrow beauty ideals and normative notions of femininity have the power to influence and possibly harm the women consuming them by skewing their body image. But feminist writers have offered different models. Revisiting these debates, Katariina Kyrölä suggests that instead of thinking of images as having an effect on passive consumers, we should conceptualize the relationship between bodies and images as a zone of *encounter*, or an interface bringing together social norms and lived experiences. Understood in this vein, body image is "a dynamically forming zone of postures that we take towards images and the world, postures we take towards ourselves and others in ways that are informed by media imageries around us" (Kyrölä, 2014: 20). This different approach moves us away from seeking evidence of causality or attempting to precisely measure effects – but it still recognizes the importance of images, that yes, they *do* matter, and in highly embodied ways.

In public debates about sexualization, young human beings are assumed to be blank slates, innocent and pure, with no sexuality of their own, until the media injects sexual ideas into them. This is, again, a particular frame – and not a very convincing one. Reputable models of healthy sexual development acknowledge that young people are, in fact, sexual in particular, age-appropriate ways (McKee et al, 2010). Following Kyrölä, media depictions of gender and sexuality contribute to body image as ways of sensing and making sense of the world, tinting and shaping it. The question then is, what kinds of sexuality, or sexiness, are being depicted, how and for whom?

In our discussion of theories of objectification we keep circling around and returning to a central point – that sex is not the same thing as sexism, even under patriarchy. Acting sexy does not therefore automatically make someone an object. We make a firm argument for the importance of sexual subjectivity, also known as agency, and the imperative of foregrounding considerations thereof in feminist inquiry. This has fundamental implications for how the notion of objectification can be used and what possibilities and limitations it involves.

In the theories of the gaze that we discussed in Chapter 2, a tradition of thinking describes the possibility of women taking agency in the way they present themselves and act as sexual subjects. In social psychology, sexual subjectivity and sexual agency refer to knowing what you want sexually, and being able to ask for it – surely a valuable civic skill for anyone, independent of their gender. This involves an "entitlement to pleasure [and] efficacy in achieving sexual pleasure", feeling "confident and in control in the sexual domain" (Horne and Zimmer-Gembeck, 2005: 25–6). Sexual agency then refers to "a sense that an individual has a right to create and take action on his or her own behalf, to make sexual choices, and to meet his or her sexual needs" (Horne and Zimmer-Gembeck, 2005: 29). Surveys have shown that women with higher levels of sexual subjectivity had "higher levels of sexual self-awareness, and lower levels of sexual anxiety ... higher self-esteem, were more resistant to sexual double standards, and scored lower on self-silencing in intimate relationships" (Horne and Zimmer-Gembeck, 2005: 28)

Sexual subjects also answer positively to questions such as "I am confident that a romantic partner would find me sexually attractive", "I am confident that others will find me sexually desirable", "I think it is important for a sexual partner to consider my sexual pleasure" and "I think about my sexuality" (Horne and Zimmer-Gembeck, 2006: 132). Looking at the attempts to define and measure sexual objectification, as addressed in the previous chapters, a clear separation between sexual agency, or subjectivity, and sexual objectification starts to grow convoluted indeed. If one is confident about a partner finding oneself attractive and sexually desirable, does this not mean objectifying oneself for another's desiring, evaluating gaze? Where, indeed, does object-ness and subject-ness begin or end, and where do they meet?

For some critics, this distinction is not truly a meaningful one, given that female sexual subjectivity is enacted in a sexist society that allows few ways out of its male-dominated logic. The feminist psychologist Sharon Lamb, for example, writes that the concept of sexual subjectivity "encourages girls to be more 'male' in the stereotyped way the culture understands the male/female sexual dichotomy" (Lamb, 2010: 299). She worries that encouraging women to understand their sexual pleasures and to ask for what they want sexually ignores whether or not those sexual practices are ethical: "If the gold standard of whether an act of sexuality is good or not is whether she experiences pleasure, then all sorts of problematic and unethical forms of sex will fall under the category of good sex (e.g. it is wrong and doesn't make sense to weigh a rapist's pleasure against a victim's harm)" (Lamb, 2010: 299). She is further concerned that to focus only on sexual agency means that we would have to say that it's OK for women to enjoy "lap-dancing and breast-flashing": "if these experiences are pleasurable, would that then make these forms of self-objectification right or good in an ethical or personal sense ... while sexual pleasure is a right it is important to be wary of views that describe all pleasures as good" (Lamb, 2010: 299–300).

This warning against sexual agency as the focus of attention is similar to the points addressed in Chapter 4 – namely the worry that some women have the *wrong* kinds of sexual agency – but Lamb also raises a more philosophical concern: that the very idea of sexual subjectivity is too limiting: "When teen girls are encouraged to be subjects not objects, those who advocate this kind of positioning run the risk of presenting only two types of sexual ways of being, object vs. subject" (Lamb, 2010: 299). She argues that sexual agency is too selfish, and that women should instead "give as well as ... receive ... seek pleasure within and from without ... love, have sex or play, with an eye towards fairness and an underlying ethos of caring and compassion" (Lamb, 2010: 303).

While Lamb makes a claim for sex and play – that is, for experimenting with forms of sex for the sheer pleasure of it – she is ultimately more interested in women partaking in "positive" sex acts defined by caring and compassion: to "become a true partner in relation to another person" in loving, coupled relationships (Lamb and Peterson, 2012: 705). We note in passing that the model of positive sex acts in this feminist approach are, in fact, somewhat similar to the positive model of sexuality offered by conservative Christianity – which brings us back to the affiliation of feminist activists and right-wing groups addressed in Chapter 3. In this model, the very idea of sexual agency is suspect because it implies the selfish, hedonistic pursuit of pleasure for which one's partner ultimately serves as an instrument, and hence object, of some kind.

For this philosophical model, the correct response to a concern that women are seen as sexual objects is to destroy the subject/object binary completely. This is entirely valid, and an overall argument that we agree with, yet we are not sure exactly what that means in terms of debates about the sexualization and objectification of women. If it simply means that women should pay less attention to their own sexual pleasure and more to that of their partners, we of course disagree – and we doubt this to be Lamb's exact point, either. In patriarchal cultures where at the last heterosexual encounter 91.9 percent of men but only 66.2 percent of women had an orgasm (Rissel et al, 2014), arguing that there should be less focus on women's pleasure would be perverse – and not in a good way. We agree with Deborah Tolman (2012), who responded to Lamb by pointing out that sexual subjectivity is not necessarily selfish – it just means knowing what you want and being able to express that. What you want and what you express can be profoundly kind, generous and thoughtful, yet it need not entail emotional commitment or any kind of relationship format. This means acknowledging that partners having sex are sexual subjects who may reciprocally objectify one another as instruments or sources of pleasure. In other words, the object/subject dichotomy simply does not stand.

Showing off

Drawing analytical distinctions between being looked at (as an object of the male gaze) and exercising agency (as a sexual subject) is convoluted at best. This book argues for a more complex understanding where people are understood simultaneously as sexual subjects and as sexual objects: that is, we both act and are acted upon, and it is through such engagements and interactions that we enact sociability, build relationships and bonds with one another, and change over time in doing so. We further argue that, as the existing scholarship examined in the preceding chapters shows, while it is hard indeed to identify instances of objectification at the level of representation, this has not stopped many from attempting to do so.

Consider Ariana Grande, a major pop star whose main fan base is made up of girls and young women. In design and content, her website arianagrande.com aims to appeal to a female audience, as do her songs with titles such as "God is a Woman" and "No Tears Left to Cry" and her pink and lilac sweatshirts, heart shaped cushions and perfume merchandise. We could argue this is evidence of a gendered mode of address that aligns with Luce Irigaray's assertion of femininity as a patriarchal system of signification (see Chapter 2). However, like a generation of female pop performers before her, we can also see Grande playing with and subverting these potentially oppressive symbols. Grande's knowing use of the symbols of femininity is clear in "7 Rings" – a song that unexpectedly borrows from *The Sound of Music*'s "My Favourite Things" while also referring to the Tiffany rings Grande bought for her friends when her engagement came to an end (see Figure 6.1).

The video for the song is set at a rowdy house party in an American suburban home. It opens with a shot of Grande looking at the camera with her mouth half open, her eyes indicating both a

Figure 6.1 Ariana Grande in "7 Rings" (2019)

challenge and something of a promise. The following shots show young women – many of whom are Grande's friends – similarly engaging with the camera while running their hands across their chests. The video, bathed in a fluorescent pink glow, shows Grande and a troupe of women dance inside and outside the house as she sings of "Girls with tattoos who like getting into trouble, lashes and diamonds, ATM machines, buy myself all of my favourite things". The song speaks of conspicuous consumption ("I see it, I like it, I want it, I got it") and the equally conspicuous artifice of her sexualized femininity: "You like my hair? Gee thanks I just bought it". Grande's overt display of feminine sexuality is underscored through lyrics that advise us "Wearing a ring but not cause I'm no Mrs, bought matching diamonds for 6 of my bitches, I'd rather spoil my friends with all my riches".

The body aesthetics are young, female and fit, rich in bared midriffs and lip gloss, with shots of Grande on all fours intersecting with those of Japanese toys emanating cuteness (or, *kawaii*). Parading themselves in corsets, pink faux fur, active wear, platform shoes and miniskirts, Grande and her dancers actively offer themselves for visual consumption, citing codes and conventions of girly femininity and sexiness, casually twerking away while giving the camera a firm look.

Ariana Grande's video performance in "7 Rings" plays with signifiers of social class, generation and ethnicity. Grande describes herself as Italian-American and the social and cultural markers out of which her iconography and stardom are fashioned are all inflected with an ethnicity and an agency that resists White Anglo-Saxon Protestant (WASP) norms and values. In part this can be attributed to Grande's rise to fame as a child star on Nickelodeon playing a stereotypical character and her reactions to the sexism and double standards of the media reportage of her private life. It also reflects the ways in which as a performer and as a media figure Grande offers, even in the most commercialized sense, an opposition to ideas of femininity and feminism that are grounded exclusively in the white experience.

As in Cindy Sherman's photography discussed in Chapter 2, the video is entirely devoid of men, calling into question how we witness this extravagant display and performance of female sexuality, consumption and excess. Here is a video made to sell the music of a female performer with a majority female fan base, revelling in the signifiers of femininity, perhaps as a route to autonomy, agency and female friendship (Grande herself has described the song as a "friendship anthem"), while also highlighting their artificiality through skewed Barbie aesthetics. This is achieved, however, through a sexualized mise-en-scène and performance register that complicates whose point of view we as an audience are meant to be witnessing this spectacle from. Are we the dispensed with man, taunted by Grande's preference for diamonds and female friendship over heterosexual bonding or are we Grande's friends enjoying ourselves freed from the shackles of performing for the pleasure of men – or both, or neither? This example – in many ways not at all exceptional – illustrates the depth of meaning that can be extracted from this kind of material and the complexity of the ways in which looking and being seen is structured in popular culture.

To simply read the video as a symptom of sexualized culture or an example of the male gaze would, in short, mean cutting several corners short. Yes, Grande's performance is steeped in sexiness, from twerks to seemingly inviting glances. Directed by Hannah Lux Davis, featuring women only, and targeted at Grande's female fans, the video does not fit easily into models of a three-fold male gaze à la Mulvey: it is not made by men; it does not feature shots of men looking at women; the main audience is not male. The sexiness performed in the video does not communicate male heterosexual desire in any direct way. Grande's videos, "7 Rings" and, even more so, "Side to Side" (2016) set in a fantastic gym and featuring thongs, half-clad and writhing bodies galore, are markedly and intentionally sexy. Whether they are sexist, and how, is a much more difficult question.

Convoluted agency

We started this book by looking at the analyses and critiques of objectification that conflate it with sexual oppression, and insist on a clear binary view of gender, culture and power. According to these, all people can be divided into one of two groups – men and women. Men are powerful; women powerless. Men look; women are looked at. We have challenged this idea throughout the book. Similarly, we reject the simple binary that one must either say that women have total control and choice over their own sexuality or return to older models of victimhood in which women are objects to which male sexuality is applied.

As we have noted, the consistent focus of sexualization reports on work emerging from social psychology has excluded research emerging from other academic traditions. Feminist writers from a variety of disciplines have worked on developing new ways of thinking about media, gender and sexual subjectivity. These approaches have complicated the simple binary of absolute agency or absolute victimhood. Writers in other disciplines have developed more complex and historically grounded notions of subjectivity in order to identify how people narrate and make meaning around their own subjective experiences of sexuality (Fahs and McClelland, 2016).

For example, drawing on the idea of a growing "new sexism" evident in postfeminist "lad culture" in which feminism was presented as having achieved its goal, Rosalind Gill argued that there was a "deliberate re-sexualisation and recommodification of bodies" that relied on depictions of women as "knowing, active and desiring", marking a shift from "an external male judging gaze to a self-policing narcissistic gaze" (Gill, 2003: 104). This warns us that just as we must not reject the possibility of female sexual agency completely, we must also avoid another extreme, of arguing that women are completely free of all structural issues and can make whatever choices they want. For, clearly, the issue is more complex: we are products of the culture that we produce, yet we do not merely reproduce it but perform variations thereof, testing out and pushing boundaries, and generate new meanings and relations by playing and rearranging elements of culture.

This is, then, not the same thing as returning to "media effects", where the media injects ideas into passive consumers. Gill's approach emphasizes women's own investments and desires rather than externally imposed ideals, "effects" or forms of copying (Gill, 2008). Developing the idea of a "postfeminist sensibility" Gill noted the appearance of a confident female figure representing women as "sexual subjects who choose to present themselves in a seemingly objectified manner" and a form of sexiness characterized by "choice, empowerment, self-surveillance ... articulated in an ironic and knowing register" (Gill, 2007a: 271), not as a "passive, objectified sex object" but as "knowingly playing with her sexual power" (Gill, 2007b: 148). This figure embodied women's pleasure and sophistication, offering a respectable, tasteful but playful model of sexiness. Gill points to new stereotypes such as the "yummy mummy" and "midriff" (also known as the "fun, fearless female") (Gill, 2008) as embodying these new trends. Gill argues that these kinds of development have become more deeply embedded over time, in media representations and the use of media to communicate and present the self, for example in the aesthetic labour involved in using filters and apps for monitoring and improving appearance (Gill, 2017: 615–20). Ariana Grande's video performances similarly speak of this sensibility, playing with stereotypes and tropes of sexiness and balancing objectification with sexual subjectivity.

The work required in the creation of glamour increasingly combines work done directly on the body with "the making and dissemination of digital images that represent the glamorised self" (Jones, 2016: 133). It is bound up with the emergence of a makeover culture (Jones, 2008) which emphasizes that "bodies, selves and environments must be in constant states of renovation, restoration, maintenance and improvement" (Jones, 2016: 132). Central to this culture is a new conception of the relations between media and bodies in which the self and the body are no longer understood as separate from representation, but instead are intertwined with images; "media-bodies" (Jones, 2008) that are "neither fully fabricated nor fully connected to fleshy life" but "part of two worlds" (Jones, 2013: 31). Images also become important means of communication and of creating bonds in the context of digital media

(Messaris, 2012; Zappavigna, 2016). Approaches such as this allow us to acknowledge that nobody – of any gender – has absolute freedom in deciding how they will make sense of their bodies and their sexualities, processes which always occur in relation to and within the cultures in which we live. But at the same time, we must acknowledge the ways in which human creativity, performance, intelligence and decision-making contribute to these processes on levels both individual and collective.

In this way of thinking about media and body, sex takes on a new significance; no longer so definitively linked to the idea of genital practices or fixed sexual identities. Eroticism becomes more free-floating, capable of being linked to other substances, emotions and activities (Bauman, 1999: 26) and appearing to permeate important aspects of contemporary life. In the context of makeover culture it signifies the capability to attract and compel the attention of others, to be *seen*. Because of this, the way that successful self-presentation is measured increasingly incorporates elements of sex appeal and sexiness and the erotic is bound up with the way we understand a person's "beauty", "charisma" and "personality". It is perhaps not surprising then, that sexualization has increasingly become a form of shorthand used to draw together a wide variety of concerns – not only about traditional media and body image, but about body work, celebrity, performance, image-making and self-representation.

Above all, though, digital media have emerged as the key focus of concern where sexualization is involved because of the forms of looking, modes of self-representation and possibilities for communication these have opened up. So for example, while emerging anxieties around sexting have much in common with earlier concerns about images of women and girls, it is "precisely their digitally mediated nature" and the fact that they "can be circulated easily around digital networks, consensually or not, contextualised or not" (Dobson, 2018) that has become a focus of debate. The creation of online fan forums, blogs, tumblrs and vlogs for sexual education, play and representation has also aroused concern as well as excitement about the new possibilities they offer. Many new kinds of sexual presentation (such as in alternative, indie, queer, feminist and amateur pornographies) and of sexual interaction (for example, in the use of contemporary hook up apps) have emerged, further complicating earlier concerns about sex, gender and representation.

These concerns are further complicated, as well as challenged, through consideration of additional axes of difference beyond that of gender which, in its often binary articulations, is a structuring element cutting through debates on objectification. While Grande's performances already point to resistance to WASP forms of feminine respectability, what happens when racial differences and gender diversity are brought to the centre in considering ways of seeing and being seen, performing sexiness or doing sex? This is what we move on to consider in Chapter 7.

7   Beyond the binary

As noted in Chapter 3, binary theories of gender and power fail to take account of intersectionality, namely the ways in which different identities work together in the play of power without being reducible to one axis of difference – oftentimes gender – above any others. We can make the same point about "the male gaze" and theories of representation and gendered power, as addressed in Chapter 2, and it is our argument that this line of questioning unsettles some of the firm, strong theory on which debates on objectification have been built. By addressing racial differences, sexual diversity and gender variance in popular media, this chapter seeks ways out from the binary logic that debates on sexual subjects and objects, the bearers of the look and the looked-at-ness-of the female objects, all entail.

Oppositional gazes, sexy black bodies

Black theorists in particular have been harsh in their critiques of theories of the gaze that assume that all women are represented in the same way, and that all men look at them in the same way. For her part, bell hooks takes issue with what she sees as the reductive nature of white feminism's concerns with the construction of femininity: "Are we really to imagine that feminist theorists writing only about images of white women, who subsume this specific historical subject under the totalizing category 'woman,' do not 'see' the whiteness of the image?" (hooks, 1992: 256) For hooks, an oppositional (intersectional) gaze is possible by noting that, "Black female spectators, who refused to identify with white womanhood ... created a critical space where the binary opposition Mulvey posits of 'woman as image, man as bearer of the look' was continually decon-structed" (hooks 1992: 258–9). For hooks, black women's critical spec-tatorship is disruptive in its "reading against the grain" and yields resistant pleasures in refusing culturally dominant images, the ways of looking at them, and the structures of power that they are embedded in.

hooks goes on to assert that not only is a critical black female spectatorship possible but its resistance is a subversion of both strategies of normative control and feminist critiques of objectifica-tion (hooks, 1992: 261). Intersectionality offers a means of under-standing how whiteness and Eurocentric conceptions of the world have been constructed as normative and superior while non-white perspectives and cultural practices are presented as deviant and inferior, part of the "technologies of control" identified by Patricia Hill Collins whereby "Whites had the power to pinion all Blacks with the power of the White gaze" (Collins 2008: 76).

As numerous critiques have made clear, the white gaze has turned a particularly exoticizing and sexualizing eye on the black body, making it the bearer of racialized myths and codes intended to reg-ulate and disempower (e.g. Hobson, 2018; Lee, 2010; Tate, 2012; Yancy, 2008). Black men and women are often reduced to contra-dictory stereotypes: objects of fear and fascination and black women, in particular, have had to bear with the "double jeopardy" (Beal, 1979 [1970]) of racism and patriarchy where they are por-trayed as hypersexual, transgressive, angry, primitive.

We can see the way that race in particular complicates the simple binary of male gaze/female object by looking at music videos produced by black female performers. Rana A. Emerson (2002) argues that music, particularly rap, has offered black women opportunities to return the gaze and re-appropriate the black female body in order to express sexual subjectivity that exceeds the bounds of white, bourgeois femininity. Indeed, black female musicians have struggled to create their own rhetorics and performances of black femininity going back to at least the early decades of the twentieth century – as we can hear in the lyrics of Lucille Bogan's "Shave 'em Dry" or "B.D. Women's Blues" recorded in 1935 (Wald, 2015). And of course performers from Josephine Baker to Rihanna have often represented "extreme, dis-proportionate sexuality" (White, 2013) where their blackness makes them objects of desire but also objects of potential disgust for white (male and female bourgeois) viewers and commentators.

Black female singers have often performed a kind of femininity that is both sexual and (from the perspective of concerned white moralists) incredibly aggressive (e.g. Coy, 2014). For example, Azealia Banks's 2011 release "212" was accompanied by a monochrome video that offered "powerful, almost predatory gestures of both sex and power" establishing "Banks as dominant ... assert[ive of] her subjectivity and allow[ing] her to directly address the gaze of the viewer." (McNally, 2016: 62). The video amplified (McDonald, 1997) the lyrics of the song which asserted Banks's pleasures in sex (particularly cunnilingus), gave her two submissive males as fellow performers and repeatedly used the word "cunt" in both visual and lyrical form – not as a profanity or a derogatory term but in order to:

> validate the black female body, challenge heteronormative norms in hip-hop, and establish herself as a figure of power ... Banks's prominent and provocative use of the word "cunt" reclaims a term men commonly use to disparage women and rearticulates it as a figure of strength and control ... her use of "cunt" permits her to reassert her sexuality on her own terms ... she has characterized the word as empowering: "To be cunty is to be feminine and to be ... aware of yourself. Nobody's fucking with that inner strength and delicateness."
>
> (McNally, 2016: 65, quoting Nika, 2012)

Seizing the iconography of the cunt goes a step further in Janelle Monáe's 2018 self-love anthem "PYNK" which memorably sees her and her dancers dressed in pink, ruffled, vulva pants standing in line with their legs apart, forming a seven-woman-strong meta depiction of a vulva. Later in the video sees one woman in "sex cells" knickers from which her pubic hair pushes out while another poses in a pair that say "I grab back" in an explicit riposte to the horrors of President Donald Trump's misogyny (and his claim on an Access Hollywood tape, made circa 2005, that, if men are famous and powerful enough, they can do whatever with and to women, including grabbing "them by the pussy"). Janelle said of the video: "PYNK is the colour that unites us all, for pink is the colour found in the deepest and darkest nooks and crannies of humans everywhere."

Nicki Minaj's much-discussed "Anaconda", released in 2014, arguably effected a similar reclamation of the "butt" (see Figure 7.1). Rappers have been singing the praises of "the bubble" ever since Sir Mix-a-lot's "Baby Got Back" hit the charts in 1992, but praise for the big booty was not without its exploitative elements and concomitant critiques (we would note here only that while "Baby Got Back" is often used as an example of the kinds of objectifying and sexist imaginary of contemporary music video, this ignores its body-positive repositioning of black women's bodies as desirable in the face of beauty standards which place whiteness and white bodies at their apex). Minaj's video, set in the steamy heat of the jungle, takes on the fetishizing gaze with a demonstration of the uniquely mesmerizing elements of twerking, while her song explicitly references the racist and sexist words spoken by the Valley Girls on the original Mix-a-lot track:

> Oh. My. God.
> Becky, look at her butt.
> It. Is. So. Big.
> She looks like one of those rap guys' girlfriends …
> they only talk to her because she looks like a total prostitute …
> I mean her butt is just so big. I can't believe it's just so round, it like, out there.
> I mean gross. Look! She's just so … black!

Minaj and her girls gyrate on chairs to the repetition of the first two lines, kicking out their legs and staring down the camera such that

Figure 7.1 Nicky Minaj and dancers in "Anaconda" (2014)

their defiance of white beauty standards is palpable. The male butt worship of "Baby Got Back" is drawn into a conversation in which Minaj takes control – the lap dances, twerking and other dance moves are tightly stage managed, shots are cut to the rhythms of the music score so that the camera does not get to linger, and its close ups are never so close that Minaj becomes "just" her body. The video is definitely spectacular but Minaj retains control of that spectacle, there is no denying her physicality, her talents, her assertiveness and her sexual agency.

Banks, Monáe and Minaj are not alone in combining combative lyrics and dance moves in order to challenge the iconographies of the "regulated" sexy body – Lizzo and CupcakKe, for example, are both extremely clear (aurally and visually) that they love their curves ("my ass is not an accessory") while refusing to shame other body types. Megan Thee Stallion takes pornographic tropes such as the pizza delivery guy and the fancy French maid to rework them, in the video for "Freak Nasty" (2018) as a paean to women's triumph over the standard assumptions that display is an indicator of sexual availability. In "Big Ole Freak" (2018), Megan cavorts in bubble baths, rubber outfits and thigh-length boots, flaunting her sexual libido and demonstrating her control of it (Dunn, 2008). That control is signified in Megan's arch engagement with the camera, alongside a camp styling of her costumes and the mise-en-scène, which reconfigure the visual imaginaries of independent, empowered female identity.

Videos like these demonstrate the problem with theories of "the male gaze" which insists that female performance is always an expression of subordination. We note that while white feminist writers such as Maddy Coy are appalled by the "pornographic performances" of black women in music videos (Coy, 2014: 4), black feminist writers have been far more open to the possibility that these performances are active, show agency and represent women taking control of the way in which they are represented. Intersectionality draws our attention to the fact that there is not one single "feminist" perspective on the representation of women.

Breasts and complicated gazes

> In line at the supermarket, a freak on the tabloid cover or the sensational photo of a murder victim lures our hapless eyes, trumpeting

harsh evidence of the randomness of human embodiment and our own mortality. We may gaze at what we desire, but we stare at what astonishes us.

(Garland-Thomson, 2009: 13)

All in all, academic research on the power relations involved in looking continues to evolve. For example, Rosemarie Garland-Thomson's analysis moves beyond the "men look at women; women watch themselves being looked at" binary by drawing attention to the practice of "staring" as an important element of our social relations. Staring occupies an ambivalent place in culture, because "people simply just don't like to be stared at"; staring can be a guilty pleasure but also inappropriate and embarrassing, for both the starer and the staree (Garland-Thomson, 2009: 5). Garland-Thomson suggests that staring is not like the gaze, the gaze possesses the one being looked at but staring has a "hidden vitality" (ibid: 9), one which might enable rethinking the status quo. Gender is one of the main ways we make sense of people and "the appearance of breasts make women legible as women", but at the same time these "ubiquitous cultural icons" (ibid: 141) engender "deep cultural ambivalence [that] turns the female breast into a perpetual peep show" (ibid: 144–5). We can illustrate this point using the work of Lizzo, a black female music performer who in the video for her song "Tempo" doesn't just entice us to gaze at her breasts – she insists on us staring at them (see Figure 7.2). So far so ordinary, perhaps. As Garland-Thomson observes:

Figure 7.2 Lizzo in "Tempo" (2019)

The social ritual of breast staring reiterates two fundamental lessons for man. First looking at breasts reminds man of what he is not. Second, looking at breasts reminds man that he can and must get what he is not. Starers see the iconic breast as abundant and available, but always only for others, not the woman herself.

(ibid: 146)

Lizzo certainly offers her breasts as abundant – she is, without doubt, abundant in every sense – but she doesn't present herself as available. Demanding a tempo she can dance to, Lizzo advances on the camera, pushes her fake-fur coat back off her breasts, and sings "Pitty-pat, pitty-pat, pitty-pitty-pat (pat)" as she taps her glitter-bikini-clad breasts in a two-handed move that sends them wobbling and sparkling. The pattern on her bikini top resembles two large eyes staring back as she processes through her dance routine, so that as we stare, we give the video, and more particularly Lizzo, "a story [and] whatever that story may be, it will not be the same one that start[ed] us staring" (Garland-Thomson, 2009: 7), not least when Lizzo starts to play her flute. Here is a woman who doesn't play by the rules (a flute in a rap video?), who isn't afraid of her own body, whose body is clearly a means of pleasure for herself. As Missy Elliott enters the scene – jumping from under the bonnet of the car to the line "fuck it up to the tempo!" – we're reminded of a longer history of black women's bodily display and musical performance. Lizzo and Missy dance together, one scantily clad, the other old skool styling a tracksuit, they holler to camera:

If you see a hater, tell him quit (stop)
Get your own dough (own dough)
Get your bread, own dough (own dough)
Go head ladies, head to the floor (floor)
Fuck up the tempo, thick girls get low (woo)

Rather than condemn this as just more sexualization and objectifica-tion, Garland-Thomson's concept of the stare allows us to think how visual interaction enables us to see the new forms of meaning and communication Lizzo's black, thick body offers. Lizzo *owns* her breasts through her defiant and inspiring body confidence and she reconfigures what it means to be sexy – her "twerk skills up on legendary". As a visual interaction, staring doesn't just reveal and define the staree, it also reveals and defines the starer. The stare is productive:

> Contradiction between the desire to stare and the social prohibitions against it fills staring encounters with angst that can be productive, leading starers to new insights. Triggered by the sight of someone who seems unlike us, staring can begin an exploratory expedition into ourselves and outward into new worlds. Because we come to expect one another to have certain kinds of bodies and behaviours, stares flare up when we glimpse people who look or act in ways that contradict our expectations.
>
> (ibid: 6)

Hence, staring cannot be thought of as just a negative action or a form of restrictive surveillance. For Garland-Thomson, staring is a visual exchange that takes us beyond simply looking, as well as beyond ideas of the gaze. It remains important to open up considerations of visual exchange beyond these two influential modes of seeing and being seen in order to acknowledge their multiplicity and shifting registers. Elizabeth Grosz (2006: 108) similarly argues for opening ways of looking beyond the gaze to modes such as the "seductive fleeting glance", "laborious observation", "a sweeping survey" and "the wink and the blink". These all entail different degrees and qualities of attention, interest and temporality, dictating "how objects are seen and even which ones are seen" (Grosz, 2006: 109). The gaze, premised on visual control, can be seen as one form of seeing among others. Furthermore, the gaze can also be conceptualized as a more complex, interactive dynamic than one premised on a binary division between the object and the subject, the passive and the active party. For, as Cahill (2011: 30) points out, the "gazer is not only active; the gazed upon is not only passive; both are bound up in a dynamic interaction that endows their subjectivity with particular characteristics and traits." In order to see and understand objects differently, we need a broader vocabulary for describing how we look, and see, in the first place.

All of these approaches suggest new ways of thinking about the complexity of power relations involved in representing and looking.

Of course, we must never forget the structural contexts within which we work. Patriarchy is real. A series of institutions and discourses work to divide men and women into separate groups and to allocate to those groups different characteristics and different values. The material objects of bodies exist in, and live in, and are made sense of, in relation to those institutions and discourses. The authors of this book insist on these truths. But we reject the suggestion that this leads us automatically to a series of simple binaries whereby men look and are powerful; women are looked at and are powerless. Philosophical models can cope with more complexity than this; and research into individual case studies shows us how, in actual women's lives, negotiations, argument and power struggles are carried out against, and through, representation.

Prance, my queen!

Recently there has been widespread address to issues of LGBTQI representations across film and television and the identification of various tropes such as the sissy, sad young man, mannish lesbian and predatory queer (see Richardson, Smith and Werndly, 2013; Kagan, 2017). Alongside exploration of how print and news media contribute to negative and outdated stereotypes and annihilation by talking *about* LGBTQI people, rather than talking to them, and acts of symbolic violence by only considering LGBTQI stories as newsworthy where they identify and can blame sexual minorities, thereby reproducing "social relations and arrangements … deemed normal, natural and inevitable" (Gill, 2007a: 114). The key thing here is that visibility can be a double-edged sword: the lack of visibility may well contribute to inequalities but visibility can be, and in the case of LGBTQI has often been the case, used to signal deviance in order to justify inequality. The mere fact of being visible cannot be equated to being seen, let alone valued – after all, "if representational visibility equals power, then almost-naked young white women should be running Western Culture" (Phelan, 1993: 10). Representation is important to social and political status but visibility alone will not guarantee constructive representations for minority groups.

Consider, for example, *RuPaul's Drag Race* (2009–), which has, over a decade, grown from a small-scale television show to an international media phenomenon spanning performance tours and special shows. The franchise is headlined and coined by RuPaul who rose to fame in the 1990s with his musical work and who has since been credited with mainstreaming drag to a broadly recognized and appreciated field of popular culture, growing into the most commercially successful drag performer ever. In feminist critique, male drag has long been a contested topic associated with sexism and misogyny. Following this line of argumentation, Kelly Kleinman (1999), has argued for an expansive condemnation of male drag as kin to racist blackface practices:

> a whole range of activities, from vaudeville "illusionists" to the pantomime dame, from *Mrs. Doubtfire* to *La Cage aux Folles*, from cross-dresser balls in Harlem to Hasty Pudding theatricals at Harvard, represent institutionalized male hostility to women on a spectrum running from prescription of desired behavior to simple ridicule. These performances may be glamorous or comic, and presented by gay men or straight men. Nonetheless, all of them represent a continuing insult to women, as is apparent from the parallels between these performances and those of white performers of blackface minstrelsy.
>
> (Kleinman, 1999: 669)

In this argument, no contextual distinctions are drawn between mainstream Hollywood films, cross-dressing within US fraternity culture or subcultural gay male drag, all of which become examples of sexist or misogynistic culture disparaging the experiences and lives of women – a form of "kicking down". Such blanket rebuttals of drag have been countered by analyses foregrounding its deconstructive and parodic capacities to denaturalize and hence to critique the gender performances and heterocentric norms that it plays with (e.g. Moore, 2013; Rupp, Taylor and Shapiro, 2010). For its part, *RuPaul's Drag Race*, as an evolving franchise, has been critiqued for amputating the radical edge of drag through commodification, and for flattening out its diversity and political dimensions in the process (see Edgar, 2011; Mercer and Sarson 2020). Critiquing the neoliberal ideology of *Ru Paul's Drag U*, a short-lived spin-off of *Drag Race*, in a transgender studies framework, Benny LeMaster (2015: 175) argues that it is guided by "oppositional sexism" which, contrary to traditional sexism aiming to sustain the subservient position of women "ensures that one's assigned sex, gender identity, and gender expression remain in alignment throughout time and space". In other words, in celebrating gay men's play with the props and exaggerated codes of femininity, the show is argued to keep binary cisgender division intact.

Interpretations connected to drag, to RuPaul's shows and persona abound. Sabrina Strings and Long T. Bui argue that the play with, and the bending of, markers of gender foregrounded in *Drag Race* does not extend to ways of performing race (Strings and Bui, 2014). They argue that except for "white facing", racial play is excluded from the show. This consideration of racial difference is, possibly surprisingly, something of an exception in scholarly attention paid to RuPaul. In another notable, yet drastically different analysis, Zine Magubane (2002) identifies RuPaul's pre-super-fame star image as a contemporary variation of blackface minstrelsy and the figure of "the white negro". According to this argument, RuPaul is culturally recognized as a white man in black skin, as someone who abides by the demands of white racist culture yet also exerts degrees of agency within it. It is nevertheless noteworthy that, in focusing on the dynamics of gender and sexuality, the majority of cultural commentaries on the show ignore the aspect of race altogether.

Concerned with the politics of representation in diverse ways, the analyses above explore ways of undoing and reproducing gendered or racialized norms and hierarchies in drag. It is clear that the mainstreaming of a subcultural practice happens within confines, and at the expense of some of its radical edge. We can see this in the removal of performances deemed too controversial from episodes of *RuPaul's Drag Race* – including the memorable performance by the Filipino-American Manila Luzon dressed up as a glamorous, bloody sanitary pad in *All Stars Season 4* (2018) during a "padding" challenge. At the same time, the popularity of the show on Netflix has performed as popular pedagogy in introducing some of the vocabulary and history of the 1980s queer ballroom culture into the mainstream – and, consequently, getting Jennie Livingstone's 1990s documentary film, *Paris is Burning* (examined by Judith Butler in her 1997 essay, "Gender is Burning" which looked at drag as disruptive gender performativity) into Netflix circulation and more popular consciousness.

We propose for critical analyses of the show's shortcomings to be met with considerations of the value of making a spectacle of one-self – in RuPaul making a huge spectacle of himself while also building a media spectacle celebrating the pleasures of queer play with the markers of gender, femininity and glamour. There is a risk of studies of cultural inquiry sliding into relativism where representations are deemed as "kinda subversive, kinda hegemonic," depending on context (Sedgwick and Frank, 1995: 17; Cvetkovitch, 2001: 287). Since cultural images and texts always afford multiple interpretations, such ambiguity is inbuilt in the theoretical framework deployed, and is not therefore a surprising analytical outcome. Rather than framing phenomena such as *Drag Race* as either subversive or hegemonic, or partly both, we would like to simply ask what the show, in featuring groups of gay men doing elaborate make-up, padding up and tucking their bodies, dressing in fantastic costumes, teetering on staggeringly high heels, proudly prancing onstage and meeting song, dance and acting challenges with more or less success, does to ways of doing gender and understanding performances of gender – not least as the show is consumed not only by gay men but by an extremely large audience of young, straight women. All this involves obvious pleasure taken in making a spectacle out of oneself, showing off and being seen. This is not merely the logic of the gaze but equally that of stares, glimpses, winks and blinks. Furthermore, it is worth considering how the spectacle of *Drag Race* fits with contemporary observations that gender fluidity is a growing tendency and nonbinary gender identifications are in constant growth. What may it mean for all this to be orchestrated by a black gay man now in his late fifties? And what can all this contribute to popular imageries for making sense of gender, and experiences and practices?

Black transwomen in *Tangerine*

While *Drag Race* was, for years, resistant to the participation of transwomen, the policy has changed during recent years. For transgender queens, the show poses a problem of building oneself into a woman when one is, actually, a woman – a problem also faced by female relatives participating in challenges with their sons and brothers competing in the show, who are made over as queens of family likeness. In other words, oppositional cisgender sexism (LeMaster, 2015) has given way to something altogether more ambivalent.

As we write this, it is clear that on a simple counting, the number of trans people, particularly trans women, in popular media has increased quite dramatically, but as GLAAD research demonstrates those representations are not necessarily more trans-positive or constructive for being more numerous. As Niall Richardson (2016) has indicated, mainstream media representation of trans folk often still relies on the tried and tested strategies of the freakshow, forms of "enfreakment" which sensationalize the bodies of transpeople so that they are "magnets" on which culture "secures its anxieties, questions, and needs" (Garland-Thomson, 1996: 2) while downplaying the symbolic and actual violence meted out to them. In fact, while our culture talks of abhorring violence, and particularly where violence is enacted by men on women, violence towards trans women is often presented as if somehow understandable – the current debates about whether or not transwomen should use female public toilets positions transwomen as essentially men, dehumanized as "deviant", "deceptive" and not really women (Bettcher, 2007). Framed in such ways, it becomes acceptable to humiliate transwomen as not "passing" correctly and thus reasonable targets of violence. Too often, trans people are on the front line of social concerns that the very idea of gender is undergoing change. In deploying trans people to create moral panic around bathrooms, the erasure of lesbians etc, all gendered bodies are brought into view – while the almost obsessive fascination with what might be in transfolk's pants is surely the most effective means of objectification.

Julia Serano (2016: 230) suggests that the media's "fascination with the feminization of trans women is a by-product of their sexualisation of all women". The idea of "femininity" is a form of regulation through normative standards of how a woman should look and act, and trans women can seemingly only be accepted if they meet those standards. If, as Serano observes, media depictions of trans women offer just two archetypes: the "deceptive transsexual" or the "pathetic transsexual" (Serano, 2016: 277) wherein transwomen are portrayed as "fake" women, and their secret trans status is revealed in a dramatic moment of "truth" (as in the 1993 film, *The Crying Game*, or the even more notorious 1981 film, *Dressed to Kill*), then there is certainly a lot of cultural anxiety about the destabilization of sex and gender as foundational categories on which social life is based. And a particular problem with some representations of transwomen has been the ways their bodies are presented on the viewers' terms – that is, for viewers to assess how well they have managed the transition – than on how the trans body feels for, and is experienced by, the transperson. Recently, TV shows such as *Transparent* (2014–19), *Orange Is the New Black* (2013–19) and *I Am Cait* (2015–16) have explored the experiences of transwomen through more multidimensional narratives. On film, *TransAmerica* (2005) and *The Danish Girl* (2015) have been box office hits, telling poignant and important stories. However, there remains the problem of who gets to play those characters – too often the trans role has been played by cis actors. This was not the case with *Tangerine* (2015), a film festival favourite featuring two trans actresses as leads (see Figure 7.3).

Sin-Dee Rella (Kitana Kiki Rodriguez) is just out of prison after serving 28 days, her friend Alexandra (Mya Taylor) meets her at a donut shop in Hollywood on Christmas Eve. Both are sex workers and Sin-Dee hears that her boyfriend and pimp, Chester (James Ransone) has cheated on her with "a white fish" (their slang for a white cis woman). Shot on iPhone 5s, the film is less interested in the bodies of its protagonists as spectacle than in the back stories and intimacy they share, and it offers a remarkably fresh approach to characters who would usually be confined by the camera's focus

Figure 7.3 Alexandra and Sin-Dee Rella in *Tangerine* (2015)

on their bodies as simply for prurient curiosity. What is particularly fascinating about *Tangerine*'s approach to its trans characters is its willingness to explore class, race, gender and sexuality without reducing its protagonists to "victims", "weirdos", "strange bodies" or "villains"; instead weaving a narrative of Sin-Dee's and Alexandra's agency in straitened circumstances. Even as they play black trans women sex workers (an overworked cinematic trope) they are not observed as passive victims of the sex industry.

The use of the iPhone camera plays a significant role in the storytelling in *Tangerine*, following Sin-Dee as she walks across Los Angeles pursuing her rival, while Alexandra walks around town drumming up an audience of friends to come see her perform her singing act in a nightclub. Throughout the journey, we can see that women like them are all too invisible to mainstream society – as they move around the Hollywood streets the two transwomen are mostly ignored by the other inhabitants of Tinseltown.

Public space is traditionally gendered masculine while "women are relegated to the private sphere" (Namaste, 1996: 225), however Sin-Dee and Alexandra "own" the streets they are filmed on (most likely they live on those streets). Lacking the domestic space that usually frames the feminine body, Sin-Dee is "back on the block and she's going hard!" As she stomps about West Hollywood searching for Dinah the camera dances around her, highlighting the vibrancy of the city landscape, but also highlighting Sin-Dee's own energy driven by fury, while her emotionality is countered by Alexandra's more measured affect. Together they are a "dynamic duo", and it is this partnership clearly set within trans-community that most particularly articulates both the feminine excess and black queerness that subverts the usual structures of the cinematic gaze.

While traditional representations of trans femininity too often highlight the tragedy of being "trapped in the wrong body" (Ashbrook, 2017) and, as Serano argues, the "possibility that trans women are even capable of making a distinction between identifying as female and wanting to cultivate a hyperfeminine image is never raised" (Serano, 2016: 229), *Tangerine* offers a version of transwomanhood which demonstrates the subversive power of Riviere's "masquerade" (discussed in Chapter 2; also Butler, 2002). Both women perform femininity as a series of styles – dressing up and make-up – and as forms of emotion. Sin-Dee and Alexandra use make-up and wigs to help them be read as women (potentially an important survival strategy for many transpeople) and their ability to appropriate and reappropriate the signifiers of femininity both confirms the performative nature of gender and challenges the "pathetic transwoman" stereotype. Sin-Dee is a firecracker woman whose jealousy sparks the events of the evening, while Alexandra is more quiet, and conciliatory (at least more often), than her friend. Alexandra's performance of a Doris Day song is presented as charming, heart-felt and authentic. Sin-Dee and her rival are the only people to show up at that performance (and Dinah only because she's been dragged there) so there is no rapturous applause from an audience, no redemptive triumph as might be expected in a more mainstream rendition of this story. The evening is a disappointment but nevertheless Alexandra is not a tragic figure – she is a diva on her own terms. Heteronormative ideals are challenged throughout the film, not least when Alexandra fights off a thieving trick with the words "You forget I got a dick too", thus marking the trans-body as a source of power.

Later, towards the end of the film, there is a scene of real poignancy which recognizes the standard trope of the "reveal" and rejects it wholeheartedly. Walking along the street Sin-Dee is attacked by men in a car who throw urine over her. The women dash into a laundromat to clean up, and Alexandra attempts to remove Sin-Dee's wig. Sin-Dee is visibly distraught, unwilling to surrender that signifier of her femininity, and Alexandra removes her own wig to give to Sin-Dee. The scene continues wordlessly as the women express their gratitude for each other. The "wrong body trope" is wonderfully queered here – the trans body is not for revelation, or a matter of shame, instead their trans-embodiment is a mode of care, connection, intimacy and sharing. This story, of poor trans women of colour whose lives are lived on the very margins of the Dream Factory of Hollywood, rejects forms of spectatorship which "feel superior watching people whose speech, dress, bodies, relationships and accents mark them as 'trash'" (Gamson, 1998: 16) or which mark the trans body as inauthentic. Instead, *Tangerine* affirms their lives are as full of friendship, love and beauty as they are of poverty, exploitation and drama; that rather than defying authenticity, Sin-Dee and Alexandra are refashioning "truth" through their trans identities, and creating their own stories (Prosser, 1998).

So, where might we go from here? The analysis in this chapter has not been about simply debunking or refusing concepts such as "the male gaze", or of proving theories of "objectification" wrong. Rather, we have sought to show that regimes of seeing are not as monolithic as some commentators might argue, nor is the theory as explanatory as some have claimed. Bearing in mind then that we argue for a more provisional analysis of what is currently happening in visual cultures, the examples we have focused on here are interesting to us because they speak back to the very concept of objectification – as Lizzo demands the right rhythm because she's a "thick bitch" in "Tempo" and Kehlani tells us its none of our business who she fucks in "Nunya" (2019) – it is clear that these women are not passive recipients of *any* gaze, male or female! Instead it might be more appropriate to understand contemporary viewing relations as a productive *interaction*. In our final chapter, we offer some ways forward.

8   Disturbingly lively objects

As we have shown throughout this book, objectification remains a central term in thinking about gender oppression in twenty-first century public debates – but it's not always clear exactly what people mean when they use the word, or what traditions of thought they build on in doing so. We have shown that, despite its seeming clarity, the concept of objectification is a broad one, which can refer to a range of strategies for treating people like objects, not all of which are related to sex, and not all of which are related to representation. We have traced the histories of ideas that have led to sexy representations becoming the key focus of concerns about objectification, and explored some of the limitations of these approaches. In this final chapter, we now offer some suggestions for alternative ways of thinking about objectification and strategies that we might take forward as we fight gender oppression.

Persistent discrimination

The first point we would like to emphasize as we think about the future of research on objectification involves returning to Marta Nussbaum's work quoted earlier, and to the history of second-wave feminism in order to insist that it is far from clear that sexy images of women are the most important forms of gender oppression facing us in twenty-first century Western countries. Nussbaum reminds us that, from a philosophical perspective, people may be made into objects in a whole range of ways, none of which truly depend on or necessitate one another, and none of which presume female subjects as the ones being objectified (see the discussion in Chapter 1).

Second-wave feminism fought gender oppression on a range of fronts, many of those battles still representing suitable objects of our fury – from sexual harassment and violence to workplace discrimination, equal pay and reproductive rights. The power of religious institutions, for example, which systematically treat women as second-class citizens and resist public sex education in schools – them also continuing to cover up the sexual abuse of children – is worth our attention. On a related point, the success of anti-feminist forces in holding back women's access to reproductive rights and control of their bodies, or even – as in some US states – rolling back these rights, is a fundamental element of gender oppression. The fact that many aspects of educational systems continue to reinforce gender stereotypes, so that women are still encouraged into traditionally feminine careers while men are funnelled into masculine ones is a source of righteous fury. The hypocrisy in the treatment of female politicians and the abuse meted out to them is appalling. For example, when Sanna Marin became the Prime Minister in Finland in December 2019, the British tabloid, *Daily Mail*, covered the event under the headline "A politician for the Instagram generation: World's youngest prime minister Sanna Marin, 34, of Finland shares VERY candid breastfeeding snaps and glamorous nights out on social media", illustrated accordingly. This example speaks of the persistent logic of objectification in tabloid media whereby younger women are effectively reduced to their bodies – the breastfeeding, the glamour – at the expense of political agency, expertise or authority. In this instance, Instagram practices, selfies included, are mobilized for the purpose as seeming proof of frivolousness.

As Bronstein (2011) pointed out, campaigns against pornography were able to become mainstream and successful at least in part because they allowed feminists to work alongside conservative Christians and powerful right-wing groups who in all other ways opposed women's rights. It seems to us that there may be a similar explanation for how "objectification" through sexy images has become one of the most visible and familiar forms of feminist politics in public debate. But it is not the only one.

Selfies, bodies, agency, sexiness

In terms of representation, there are more interesting and useful ways in which we can think about the relationship between sexual representation and sexy images than the dynamics of "objectification". In offering a way forward, we return to the beginning of this book and the challenge offered by selfies to our theories of representation. We noted in Chapter 1 that accusations that Kim Kardashian has turned herself into an "object" by taking selfies raise interesting questions about what an "object" is, and whether it's a bad thing to be "objectified". The same applies to the sexy performances of Ariana Grande, Nicki Minaj or Lizzo – and to the Instagram selfies of a politician like Sanna Marin.

In the early twenty-first century, selfies – self-shot photographs, usually taken at arm's length or in front of a mirror using a mobile phone – have become ubiquitous. Selfies can be taken for oneself, shared with friends or a sexual or romantic (potential) partner, shared with wider social networks or posted publicly. The decision to duckface or fishgape, smize or squinch is a signal of the democratization of portraiture, photography and publicity made possible, in part, by social media platforms such as Instagram or Snapchat. The rise of the camera phone and digital modification apps have given so-called ordinary people the power to represent themselves as glamourous, sexy, beautiful, desirable and interesting, in ways which used to be limited to those who could afford, or whose celebrity warranted, the services of professional photographers. To engage in this form of image making and sharing is often worried about as evidence of narcissism and a frivolous willingness (on the part of girls, particularly) to self-objectify (see Tiidenberg, 2018).

The critiques of selfies use terms familiar from the discourses we have mapped in this book: young women are too sexy, too concerned with appearance, they are objectifying themselves, and so on. Numerous (female) journalists and psychologists have condemned teenage girls' selfies as forms of self-absorption which belie their "struggle with low self-esteem" (Walker, 2013) and as evidence of even wider problems of social isolation, that "selfies were for people without friends" (Losse, 2013). As a recent article in the academic journal *Body Image* argued:

> Ordinary women – such as those not famous through traditional media mass outlets –are now able to create objectifying imagery for an audience to view and evaluate. Not only are selfies objectifying in general (i.e., focus on one's body as an

aesthetic object), but they also may depict thin and sexualized beauty ideals commonplace in traditional mass media.

(Vendemia and DeAndrea, 2018: 119)

Drawing on the social psychological research we have discussed in this book, which deploys objectification as a self-evident category, selfies have been presented in public discourse as exacerbating the problems of gendered looking by encouraging young women to present themselves in the "unnatural" styles of celebrities. Joining the large body of argument that claims that thin and sexualized depictions of women in mass media (such as advertising, magazines, television, movies, music videos, video games and pornography) can cause serious psychological risks and physical harm for female viewers, the selfie now takes its place as promoter of unrealistic body types and contributor to viewing the self from a third person perspective, that is, turning oneself into an object to be valued only for one's external appearance.

Such pathologizing accounts are often focused on the activities of teenagers, women and sexual minorities, which might alert us to the particular power dynamics at play, and these arguments are mostly devoid of any conception that "self-shooting" might have subtle but important significances for the people taking images of themselves. Indeed, the ways selfie practices are discussed can have a regulatory function. For example, Burns argues that discussions are often framed to:

> reflect social norms and anxieties, and [so] supports, maintains and reproduces a patriarchal authority and gendered power relations by perpetuating negative feminine stereotypes that then legitimise the social control over young women's behaviours and identities.

(Burns, 2015: 1716)

Furthermore, because selfies are constructed as a gendered practice, they can then be devalued through their association with the "feminine" qualities of vanity and triviality (see also Hendry, 2014). As in the social psychological research addressed in Chapter 5, objectification in these accounts means focusing on your body as an aesthetic object, as if appreciating one's own appearance is in itself proof of mental health problems.

Even more worrying for some commentators has been the sharing of images for sexual reasons – whether on dating apps such as Tinder or Grindr, or between people already in relationships (including both committed and casual relationships), or flirting between strangers as a prelude to something more. Worries about the commodification of the self, and of an increasingly superficial market in sexual attractiveness borrow heavily from the "science", while at the same time disavowing the moralizing about "too many partners" or "not being serious enough" about relationships. As in the radical feminist discourses that opened this book, selfies are also seen to be a problem because they buy into heterosexual, patriarchal visions of sexuality, feminine attractiveness and availability.

These discourses of objectification are common in public debates. However, as we have argued in this book, such approaches to representation are problematic because they ignore the possibility of agency, and particularly of sexual subjectivity – the ability to know what we want sexually, and to ask for it. Research that has been based on actually speaking to the young women involved about their "sexy selfie" practice, shows that there is no either/or about selfies, that girls navigate their practices of self-portraiture and sexiness in ways that both challenge and reproduce contemporary heteronormative ideas of heterosexiness (Naezer, 2018). For example, Jessica Ringrose (2011) describes girls' performances of "desirable but not too slutty" femininity through selfies. Sander De Ridder and Sofie Van Bauwel (2013) have examined the ways in which young people negotiate gender and sexualities when commenting on profile pictures in social media. They found that although commenting on pictures was a highly gendered practice, it also disrupted some norms. Furthermore, notions of feminine passivity were disrupted by girls' high participation in commenting on and communicating about each others' photos, fashion, make up, and so forth, and in the seeming ordinariness of their ability to view and comment on male bodies. Selfie exchange and the communication practices connected to it can then perform a number of functions, from creating, experimenting with and performing identity to receiving validation (Dobson, 2011; Naezer, 2018; Albury, 2015; Tiidenberg, 2018).

Marijke Naezer's (2018) ethnographic study of selfie practices among twelve to eighteen year old girls in the Netherlands showed that the ways in which girls positioned themselves, and their peers, intersected with "dominant gendered, heteronormative, racialized, classed and religious discourses about sexiness" (Naezer, 2018: 12), but also with their body shape, popularity, and perceived "smartness". For many people, posting selfies and sharing sexy images is a low-risk and enjoyable activity, and these images, as a form of display, can be about building trust, intimacy and connection (Setty 2018). What each of these kinds of audience/participant research show is that selfie-taking and image sharing are forms of communication beyond simply presenting an image that can be subjected to forms of textual analysis. Image sharing can be an expression of intimacy and trust (Albury et al, 2013; Hasinhoff, 2015; Hasinhoff, 2013) but also of ways of expressing changing meanings of the body.

It may nonetheless seem to some that selfie culture exemplifies the profound structuring force of the male gaze in women's ways of offering themselves as to be looked at. According to such a logic, self-objectification would be currently internalized as every woman's game. Despite the appeal that this line of analysis affords, "the male gaze", as presented by Mulvey, relates to specific cinematic production practices involving male institutions, directors and cameramen, as well as the positioning of women as those to be looked at by both male characters and members of the audience: it was never a general template for considering gendered relations of looking and seeing. Nor do selfies easily fit into Berger's model of seeing, in that the one taking the selfies – say, a young woman – is, in also looking at herself on the screen while posing, she chooses the images she prefers and most likely edits them before publishing any. The audience can be chosen and targeted, it may be composed of people of any gender, or there may not even be an audience beyond the selfie hobbyist herself.

It has been argued that social media allow for new forms of mediatized life enabling what boyd (2014) describes as presencing or self-production, using different media platform(s) to curate an image and/or identity (Dobson, 2011; boyd, 2014). This is both a reflexive and, crucially, a social process. While recent stories in the press have suggested that social media makes young people depressed and isolated, Waite argues that social media-based interactions are forms of "online sociality" connected to in-person "material sociality" as an extension of offline lives (Waite, 2011: 22); giving people a sense of belonging and also making visible their social connections. These activities occur across time – Lincoln and Robards explored how individuals in their early twenties revised their Facebook profiles and timelines to "realign [their] identity with new imaginings of audience (Facebook friends) and [themselves]" (Lincoln and Robards, 2016: 11). In doing this self-production, people can not only curate but also experiment with an identity, in a space that is relatively safe (Livingstone, 2008).

Drawing on Rebecca Coleman's concept of "bodies as becoming", Katrin Tiidenberg and Edgar Gómez Cruz's research opens up the possibilities that "selfie practices engage with normative, ageist and sexist assumptions of the wider culture in order to understand how specific ways of looking become possible" (Tiidenberg and Gómez Cruz, 2015). Their small-scale study demonstrates that through the interactions, community and sharing online, women's experiences of their bodies are changing and that, far from being trapped in ways of relating to the body as "objectified", practices of taking images and viewing, commenting on others enables more agentic forms of body imaging. Tiidenberg and Gomez Cruz's account moves beyond the complaints of the narrowness of the ideals on offer and, by drawing on Coleman, they also avoid the ontological separation of bodies and images that underpins the arguments that images have effects on young women's bodies as we outlined earlier. Coleman's Deleuzean research "shifts the focus of feminist empirical work (...) from questions of media cause and effect towards a consideration of how bodies are known, understood, experienced – how bodies become – through images" (Coleman, 2008: 24).

Hence we may need to rethink our understandings of objectification in relation to subject/object in the digital age, that mobile technologies offer possibilities for experimentation and reworking of the traditional hierarchies of beauty. Selfie-snapping performs the work of posing: creating the perfect smize is a skill, takes forms of knowledge – not just what light might be best but also how to move eyes, lips, chin while at the same time holding the camera at the right angle. The ability to view, discard, retake and filter the image is both a convenience and a measure of expertise, and is available to anyone to perfect in order to produce the ultimate Brow Too Strong.

In this context, acts of self-imaging such as selfies can be understood not as forms of self-objectification but as acts of cultural production (Hasinoff, 2013). Approaching them from this perspective offers a way out of a tired debate about whether women are active or passive, empowered or undermined when they engage in sexual representation. Instead of focusing on individual agency or its lack, a focus on cultural production involves considering "intimate and sexual media practices ... as potentially *valuable* forms of social and cultural capital", but ones that are also marked by inequalities of participation (Dobson, 2018: 95, see also Albury and Byron, 2014; Albury, 2015; Harvey and Ringrose, 2015). These practices may be valuable, both in themselves and as a form of social currency, but the capital they represent is accumulated differently and according to who performs them. Rather than assuming that sexual representation is in and of itself problematic, we can instead ask when and how it is judged to be successful; which kinds of representation can be converted into capital (whether social or economic) and when, instead, they work against the status of those who perform them.

Importantly, academic research on selfies shows that we do not have to choose an either/or position whereby we say that selfies prove that young women are totally empowered, or that they are helpless objects. We do not have to say that Kim Kardashian is simply an object, nor reject the fact that she is producing objects (selfies) that show her body in a sexy way. As we suggested in Chapter 7, academic research is offering more interesting and sophisticated ways to think about – and challenge – the subject/object binary.

We are objects; what kinds of objects are we?

It further remains a fact that human bodies *are* objects: we are all material objects of specific density, mass and texture that exist in a particular time and place. As Ann Cahill (2011) argues, many a feminist critique of objectification ignores the "thingness" of personhood as something always already rooted in the materiality of bodies. She then argues that "to be treated as a thing, a body, is not inherently degrading because we are, in fact, bodily things; it is only within the context of a theory of personhood that vilifies the material that such treatment becomes degrading" (Cahill, 2011: 25). This is an apt point to make, and one that is in direct friction with Rae Langton's (2009) argument that pornography silences women through dehumanization – an argument similar to that posed at length by Susan Griffin in her 1981 book, *Pornography and Silence*. But to argue that women making porn are silenced can be just another means of ignoring their voices and perspectives that may be in conflict with one's own, thereby framing women making porn as having nothing to add to feminist discussions concerning pornography.

Following on from Katherine Behar's (2016) discussion of feminist object-oriented ontology, we argue that since people are always already objects, they do not require a process of objectification to become such. Seen in this vein, the objecthood of human bodies as material entities does not simply equal or stand for dehumanization or the lack of subjectivity. The question of objects and subjects can, and should, be examined outside a binary framing, for one is not simply *either* a subject who acts *or* an object that is acted upon. People can simultaneously act as subjects and be treated as objects by others. To be objectified means to being reduced to one's physical properties – to be treated like a piece of meat. An attempt to objectify does not however necessarily stick, or have much effect, as the issue is one of both relationality and social power.

We groom our bodies, observe our shifting weight, apply makeup and deodorant, accessorize, dress, exfoliate and moisturize. Everyday lives are rife in instances and practices where we trim and stylize ourselves, as objects, in order to allow others to perceive us, and possibly to relate to us, in particular ways. We dress for occupational roles, for a night out or an evening in, regulating the ways in and the degrees to which we show off our bodies, how we make ourselves sexually or otherwise approachable, or not, and how we communicate subcultural, ethnic or religious affiliations. People of different genders, ages, ethnicities and sexual orientations create and consume representations, positioning themselves as objects of vision and desire. We may willingly occupy the role of objects in our sexual relations where it is not uncommon to momentarily occupy the role of a fetishized object.

In fact, *not being found* sexually desirable by those that one desires – that is, the failure to be pleasurably objectified – can be nothing short of a personal tragedy, given how central sexual desire, attachment and pleasure are in people's lives, independent of gender identifications or sexual orientations. As Cahill (2011: 84) argues, this is nothing less than a question concerning one's very sense of agency: "To have that gaze skip over you, to be rendered sexually invisible by society at large, is to have your full personhood denied." Following Cahill (2011: 26), to be sexual is also to be a thing and object of another's gaze. This does not presume a gender binary, or a power imbalance or passivity on the part of the one being objectified.

It thus follows that all kinds of bodies can be, and are, treated as objects, not least in the realm of sexuality, but this occurs in dissimilar and regularly complex ways. Further, being perceived by someone as an object does not automatically mean being reduced in one's agency to an instrument lacking in subjectivity – the question being one of how precisely such recognition or misrecognition occurs, and what kinds of spaces of agency all this connects with. This book has argued for an understanding of subjectivity and objecthood as coexistent, rather than as mutually exclusive. As material, embodied beings, we are object-subjects, or subject-objects acting out in the world and establishing connections with other bodies within it. There is a plethora of ways to represent, and self-represent our bodies for our own pleasure as well as for the pleasure of others, and under different sets of social constraints. We can stage ourselves as objects of visual pleasure for the purposes of flirtatious invitation, as an offer of services, or as a way of perceiving ourselves from a distance, as if through the eyes of another: none of this implies or necessitates an annulment of agency or subjectivity. Furthermore, none of these practices need be confined in a heteronormative framework premised on binary gender.

Concerns connected to agency or the lack of it, as articulated through the notion of objectification, can be framed as ones involving connections between objects – that is, as a matter of how people relate to one another, the kinds of spaces that people are given to move within, the kinds of hierarchies that are established between different bodies, as well as the diverse values that are attached to people and their actions. The issue further becomes one of the specific properties of objects and the ornamental and instrumental uses that they may be put into. All this can play out in a number of ways. Employees, for example, have an instrumental value for and role in the organizations they work for. A cleaner cleans, a cook cooks, a researcher does research, a teacher teaches and a driver drives, fulfilling a function and hence instrumental to advancing the operations in question: all are, to a certain extent, objects. Some work is more highly paid, and valued, than others. In the constant performance tracking within universities, for example, individual employees such as the authors of this book are data points whose value for the institution translates as their specified, negotiable salary level, and as continued or discontinued contracts.

As we discussed in Chapter 4, it is regularly argued that sex workers "sell their bodies", but the same principle extends to all realms of labour, which, from the obviously physical – sex work, farm labouring, mining or building – to the sedateness of office work (where bodies are impacted by the long hours of sitting and repetitive strain injuries from hunching over computers, etc), occurs under specific monetary contracts and comes with particular risks to one's physical well-being that entail negotiations as to the balance of costs and gains involved. In some occupational realms, employees have access to health benefits and private medical care, while those in more precarious labour arrangements weather their material conditions of existence without a similar support network. This literally speaks of the different value placed on the bodies in question, some of which are seen as more easily replaced than others. All this brings us back to questions concerning social relations of power.

These power relations matter and they weigh heavily upon bodies, crafting alignments, hierarchies and differentials between them. As one axis of social power, sexism casts women as beings of less stature and agency with the aim of cutting down the ability of female-identified bodies to act out in the world. Should we conflate sexism with sexual representation, as more than easily happens under the rubric of objectification, it becomes impossible to see how sexual representation can open up and sustain the agency of female bodies in discovering pleasures, in connecting with other bodies and in making sense of themselves. In a cultural moment when female nudity in particular is increasingly weeded out of social media following Tumblr's ban on "female-presenting nipples" and other offensive content in 2018, the possibilities for women to explore ways of representing themselves are being narrowed down as female nudity is simply equated with obscenity. This, we argue, is sexist.

Objectification, sexualization and the future of gender oppression

All of which brings us back to a key argument throughout this book – that sexual representation or sexiness are not the same thing as sexism, and should not be conflated with it. What then, to do with diagnoses of "sexualization" and the uses of "objectification" within them? As we have shown, the way the term has been mobilized has often been used against women, girls and LGBTQI people, working to obscure important issues of power. As Gill and Orgad (2018) argue, there are more productive terms that we can now use for describing and analyzing the changing relations of sex and media: such as mediated sexual citizenship, mediated intimacy, the quantified or datafied sexual self.

Sexualization can nevertheless be a productive term for exploring a number of issues: a contemporary fascination with sexual values, practices and identities, the growth and diversification of sexual media, the ways that pornographic styles and aesthetics have been redeployed in popular culture texts, new kinds of sexual experience, the shifting relations of commerce and intimacy, the ways that sex has become particularly visible – "onscene" – in Western culture, both as a source of leisure, entertainment and self-discovery and as a site of fascination, concern and regulation. Indeed, sexualization debates themselves can be understood as part of these developments. Understood in this vein, "sexualization" is much more than a diagnosis for harm, connected as it is to advances in sexual rights, in the representation and public participation – and not merely the visibility – of sexual minorities and subcultures, and in the overall framing of sexuality as a political issue connected to citizenship and agency. At the same time, however, predominant discourses on sexualization, such as the policy documents addressed in Chapter 6, tend not to associate such advances with female sexuality which they fail to recognise as connected to minority rights or self-presentation affording novel ways of figuring selfhood, intimacy, or community.

Critiques of sexualization have been primarily targeted at inappropriate approximations of adult sexuality in children's commodity culture, as well as against the reduction of women into sexual objects through media representations. In these, critiques of sexism blend in with concerns about sex. Rosalind Gill points out that:

> Media are contradictory locations for exploring "sexualization" since they are sites both where the phenomenon can (arguably) be observed and where it is discussed and dissected, usually as a matter of "concern". Not infrequently these two can coexist in the same space, as when newspapers and magazines print outraged or "concerned" readers' opinion pieces about toys featuring the playboy bunny or the selling to children of T-shirts bearing the legend "Future Porn Star" (to take two recent examples), amidst a range of other content (photographs of topless women, adverts for telephone sex lines and so on) which itself might attract the label "sexualized". The media, then, are paradoxically perhaps both the biggest source of "sexualized" representations, as well as the primary space where debates about "sexualization" are aired.
>
> (Gill, 2009: 140)

While this is by necessity a simplification, we suggest this paradox is connected to the tenacious heterosexism cutting through debates on female sexuality: while the figure of the gay (white, able-bodied) man occupies something of a paradigmatic position as a queer subject, public debates on women's sexuality compulsively return to heterosexual norms and presumptions, according to which sexualization and objectification are only ever processes that involve heterosexual desire and heteronormative relations. This speaks of a perceived lack of female sexual desire that presents women as passive recipients of both male sexual advances and cultural systems of representation, and infantilizes them in the process. We, however, argue for the queer feminist imperative of highlighting and foregrounding active female sexual desire and agency in ways that both challenge and refuse the position of passivity and lack on offer. This means working harder to broaden the range of ways in which women – and men, and non-binary individuals – of all sizes, generations, classes and ethnicities experience and enjoy being sexy, being sexual and taking sexual pleasure. It means foregrounding issues of consent, respect, contextual care and consideration in terms of both critical and sexual agency – even when the forms those take do not conform to one's own views and agendas.

And this is not a bad place to leave our argument, and to point towards possible future work for feminist activists fighting gender oppression.

Let's go.

References

Albury, Kath. 2002. *Yes means yes: getting explicit about female heterosex.* Crows Nest, NSW: Allen & Unwin.

Albury, Kath. 2014a. 'Porn and sex education, porn as sex education'. *Porn Studies*, 1: 172–181.

Albury, Kath. 2014b. '*Sexting, selfies and sex and relationships education in Australia*'. Paper presented at the Cultural Studies Association of Australasia Annual Conference. Wollongong. 2–5 December 2014.

Albury, Kath. 2015. 'Selfies, Sexts and Sneaky Hats: Young People's Understandings of Gendered Practices of Self-Representation'. *International Journal of Communication*, 9: 1734–1745.

Albury, Kath and Paul Byron. 2014. 'Queering sexting and sexualisation'. *Media International Australia*, 153(1): 138–147.

Albury, Kath, Kate Crawford, Paul Byron and Benjamin P. Mathews. 2013. *Young people and sexting in Australia: Ethics, representation and the law.* ARC Centre for Creative Industries and Innovation/Journalism and Media Research Centre, UNSW, Australia.

American Psychological Association (APA). 2007. 'Report of the APA Task Force on the Sexualization of Girls'. http://www.apa.org/pi/women/programs/girls/report-full.pdf, accessed 2 February 2019.

Ang, Ien. 1985. *Watching Dallas: Soap Opera and the Melodramatic Imagination.* London: Routledge.

Anon. 2019. 'Pink and White'. *CrashPadSeries.com*. 25 April 2019. https://crashpadseries.com/queer-porn/, accessed 28 April 2020.

Aronowitz, Nona Willis. 2019. 'Sex, Lies, and Andrea Dworkin'. *The Cut.* 6 March 2019. https://www.thecut.com/2019/03/sex-lies-and-andrea-dworkin.html, accessed 20 February 2019.

Ashbrook, Emily. 2017. 'How useful, if at all, is the idea of being "trapped in the wrong body" in thinking about Trans issues?'. *ANDROGYNY*, 1(2): 2–7.

Attwood, Feona. 2006. 'Sexed up: Theorizing the sexualization of culture'. *Sexualities*, 9: 77–94.

Attwood, Feona. 2009. 'Introduction: The sexualization of culture'. In Attwood, F. (ed.), *Mainstreaming Sex: The Sexualization of Western Culture*. London: I.B. Tauris, pp. xiii–xxiv.

Attwood, Feona. 2017. *Sex Media*. Cambridge: Polity.

Awkward-Rich, Cameron. 2017. 'Trans, Feminism: Or, Reading like a Depressed Transsexual: Winner of the 2017 Catharine Stimpson Prize for Outstanding Feminist Scholarship'. *Signs: Journal of Women in Culture and Society*, 42(4): 819–841.

Bailey, Reg and Department for Education. 2011. 'Letting children be children; Report of an Independent Review of the Commercialisation and Sexualisation of Childhood'. https://assets.publishing.service.gov.uk/government/uploads/system/uploads/attachment_data/file/175418/Bailey_Review.pdf, accessed 28 February 2020.

Barker, Meg and Robbie Duschinsky. 2012. 'Sexualisation's four faces: sexualisation and gender stereotyping in the Bailey Review'. *Gender and Education*, 24(3): 303–310.

Baron, Robert A. and Deborah R. Richardson. 1994. *Human Aggression*. 2nd edition. New York and London: Plenum Press.

Bartky, Sandra. 1988. 'Foucault, femininity and the modernization of patriarchal power'. In Diamond, Irene and Lee Quinby (eds.), *Feminism and Foucault: Reflections on resistance*. Boston: Northeastern Press University, pp. 61–86.

Bartlett, Alison and Margaret Henderson. 2016. 'What is a Feminist Object? Feminist Material Culture and the Making of the Activist Object'. *Journal of Australian Studies*, 40(2): 156–171.

Basiliere, Jenna. 2009. 'Political is personal: scholarly manifestations of the feminist sex wars'. *Michigan Feminist Studies*, 22(1). https://quod.lib.umich.edu/cgi/t/text/text-idx?cc=mfsfront;c=mfs;c=mfsfront;idno=ark5583.0022.101;g=mfsg;rgn=main;view=text;xc=1, accessed 28 March 2019.

Bauman, Zigmunt. 1999. 'On Postmodern Uses of Sex'. In Featherstone, Mike (ed.), *Love and Eroticism*. London: Sage.

Beal, Frances M. 1979 [1970]. '*Double Jeopardy: To Be Black and Female*'. In Bambara, Toni Cade (ed.), *The Black Woman: An Anthology*. New York: New American Library, pp. 90–100.

Behar, Katherine. 2016. 'An Introduction to OOF'. In Behar, Katherine (ed.), *Object-Oriented Feminism*. Minneapolis: Minnesota University Press, pp. 1–36.

Beirne, Rebecca. 2012. 'Interrogating lesbian pornography: gender, sexual iconography and spectatorship'. In Hines, Claire and Darren Kerr (eds.),

Hard to Swallow: hard-core pornography on screen. London and New York: Wallflower Press, pp. 229–243.

Berg, Heather. 2014. 'Labouring porn studies'. *Porn Studies*, 1(1–2): 75–79.

Berg, Heather. 2018. 'Workers and publics'. *Porn Studies*, 5(2): 217–220.

Berger, John. 1972. *Ways of Seeing*. London: Penguin Classics.

Berglund, Clara, Jenny Westerstrand, Olga Persson and Zandra Kanakaris. 2019. 'Vi behöver en lag mot skadliga sexrobotarna'. *Expressen*. 20 February 2019. https://www.expressen.se/debatt/lagstifta-mot-de-skadliga-sex robotarna/, accessed 28 February 2019.

Berlant, Lauren and Michael Warner. 1998. 'Sex in public'. *Critical Inquiry*, 24(2): 547–566.

Bernstein, Elisabeth. 2007. *Temporarily Yours. Intimacy, Authenticity and the Commerce of Sex*. Chicago: University of Chicago Press.

Bettcher, Talia. 2007. 'Evil Deceivers and Make-Believers: On Transphobic Violence and the Politics of Illusion'. *Hypatia A Journal of Feminist Philosophy*, 22(3): 43–65.

Bindel, Julie. 2009. 'My sexual revolution', *The Guardian*. 30 January 2009. https://www.theguardian.com/lifeandstyle/2009/jan/30/women-gayrights, accessed 25 November 2019.

Bonilla, Bethney. 2019. 'Interview with Shine Louise Houston, feminist pornography filmmakers'. *vwordpod.com*. https://vwordpod.com/inter view-with-shine-louise-houston-feminist-pornography-filmmaker, accessed 25 March 2019.

Braun-Courville, Debra K. and Mary Rojas. 2009. 'Exposure to Sexually Explicit Web sites and Adolescent Sexual Attitudes and Behaviors'. *Journal of Adolescent Health*, 45(2): 156–162. doi:10.1016/j.jadohealth.2008.12.004.

Boston Women's Health Collective, The. 1973. *Our bodies, Ourselves*. New York: Simon and Schuster.

boyd, danah. 2014. *It's complicated*, London: Yale University Press.

Boyle, Karen. 2010. 'Introduction: Everyday pornography'. In K. Boyle (ed.), *Everyday Pornography*. London: Routledge, pp. 1–13.

Bridges, Ana J., Robert Wosnitzer, Erica Scharrer, Chyng Sun and Rachael Liberman. 2010. 'Aggression and Sexual Behavior in Best-Selling Pornography Videos: A Content Analysis Update'. *Violence Against Women*, 16(10): 1065–1085. doi:10.1177/1077801210382866.

Brocart, Paul. 2014. 'An interview with Shine Louise Houston'. *GenERe*. https://genere.hypotheses.org/270, accessed 11 April 2019.

Bronstein, Carolyn. 2011. *Battling Pornography: the American feminist anti-pornography movement 1976–1986*. Cambridge UK: Cambridge University Press.

Burns, Anne. 2015. 'Self(ie)-Discipline: Social Regulation as Enacted Through the Discussion of Photographic Practice'. *International Journal of Communication*, 9: 1716–1733.

Busch, Noél Bridget, Holly Bell, Norma Hotaling and Martin A. Monto. 2002. 'Male Customers of Prostituted Women: Exploring Perceptions of Entitlement to Power and Control and Implications for Violent Behavior Toward Women'. *Violence Against Women*, 8(9): 1093–1112.

Butler, Jeremy. 2004. 'Police programs'. In Horace Newcomb (ed.) *Encyclopedia of Television*. New York and London: Fitzroy Dearborn, pp.1779–1783.

Butler, Judith. 1997. 'Gender is burning: Questions of appropriation and subversion'. *Cultural Politics*, 11: 381–395.

Butler, Judith. 2002 [1990]. *Gender trouble: Feminism and the subversion of identity*. London: Routledge.

Cahill, Ann. 2011. *Overcoming Objectification*. London and New York: Routledge.

Cahill, Ann. 2014. 'The Difference Sameness Makes: Objectification, Sex Work, and Queerness'. *Hypatia*, 29(4): 840–856.

Califia, Patrick. 2000. *Public sex: The Culture of Radical Sex*. Berkeley, CA: Cleis Press.

Chateauvert, Melinda. 2014. *Sex Workers Unite: A History of the Movement from Stonewall to SlutWalk*. Boston: Beacon Press.

Cixous, Helene. 1976. 'The Laugh of the Medusa'. *Signs*, 1(4): 875–893.

Clarke, D.A. 2004. 'Prostitution for everyone: feminism, globalisation and the "sex" industry'. In Stark, Christine and Rebecca Whisnant (eds.), *Not For Sale: feminists resisting prostitution and pornography*. Melbourne: Spinifex, pp. 149–205.

Coalition for a Feminist Sexuality and Against Sadomasochism. 1983. 'Leaflet distributed at Barnard Conference'. *Feminist Studies*, 9(1): 180–182.

Cole, Susan G. 1992. *Pornography and the Sex Crisis*. Toronto: Second Story Press.

Coleman, Rebecca. 2008. 'The Becoming of Bodies: Girls, Media Effects, and Body Image'. *Feminist Media Studies*, 8(2): 163–179.

Collins, Patricia Hill. 2004. *Black Sexual Politics: African Americans, Gender, and the New Racism*. New York: Routledge.

Collins, Patricia Hill. 2008. 'Reply to Commentaries: Black Sexual Politics Revisited'. *Studies in Gender and Sexuality*, 9(1): 68–85.

Collins, Patricia Hill and Sirma Bilge. 2016. *Intersectionality*. Cambridge UK: Polity.

Coy, Maddy. 2014. '"Pornographic Performances": a review of research on sexualization and racism in music videos'. Report prepared for End Violence Against Women, Imkaan and Object. http://www.preventionpla

tform.co.uk/media/Pornographic-Performances-FINAL-Aug-2014.pdf, accessed 28 July 2019.

Crenshaw, Kimberle. 1989. 'Demarginalizing the Intersection of Race and Sex: A Black Feminist Critique of Antidiscrimination Doctrine, Feminist Theory and Antiracist Politics'. *University of Chicago Legal Forum*, 1989(1): 139–167.

Crenshaw, Kimberle. 1991. 'Mapping the Margins: Intersectionality, Identity Politics, and Violence against Women of Colour'. *Stanford Law Review*, 43(6): 1241–1299.

Cvetkovitch, Ann. 2001. 'Fierce Pussies and Lesbian Avengers: Dyke Activism Meets Celebrity Culture'. In Bronfen, Elisabeth and Misha Kavka (eds.), *Feminist Consequences: Theory for the New Century*. New York: Columbia University Press, pp. 283–318.

Dawson, Kate, Chloe Cooper and Jenny Moore. 2018. '"They giggle and I crush over them": porn as pedagogy at Tate Modern'. *Porn Studies*, 5(1): 91–96.

Dean, Jonathan. 2012. 'On the March or on the Margins? Affirmations and Erasures of Feminist Activism in the UK'. *European Journal of Women's Studies*, 19(3): 315–329.

Delacoste, Frédérique (ed.). 2018. *Sex Work: Writings by Women in the Sex Industry*. Jersey City: Cleis Press Start.

de Beauvoir, Simone. 2011 [1949]. *The second sex* (C. Borde and S. Malovany-Chevallier, trans.). London: Vintage – The Random House Company.

Deeley, Laura. 2008. 'I'm single, I'm sexy, and I'm only 13'. *The Times*. 28 July 2008. https://www.thetimes.co.uk/article/im-single-im-sexy-and-im-only-13-gf3vcxpsjwh, accessed 28 October 2019.

De Fren, Allison. 2008. *The exquisite corpse: Disarticulations of the artificial female*. Los Angeles: University of Southern California.

De Fren, Allison. 2009a. 'Technofetishism and the Uncanny Desires of ASFR (alt. sex. fetish. robots)'. *Science Fiction Studies*: 404–440.

De Fren, Allison. 2009b. 'The Anatomical Gaze in Tomorrow's Eve'. *Science Fiction Studies*: 235–265.

De Ridder, Sander and Sofie Van Bauwel. 2013. 'Commenting on pictures: Teens negotiating gender and sexualities on social networking sites'. *Sexualities*, 16(5–6): 565–586.

Dines, Gail. 2011. *Pornland: How Porn Has Hijacked Our Culture*. Boston, MA: Beacon Press.

Ditum, Sarah, 2012. 'Do 63% of girls really want to be glamour models? No'. *Liberal Conspiracy*. 23 April 2012. http://liberalconspiracy.org/2012/04/23/do-63-of-girls-really-want-to-be-glamour-models-no/, accessed 17 November 2019.

Doane, Mary Ann. 1980. 'Misrecognition and Identity'. *Cine-tracts*, 3(3, Fall): 25–33.

Doane, Mary Ann. 1982. 'Film and the Masquerade: Theorising the Female Spectator'. *Screen*, 23: 74–87.

Dobson, Amy Shields. 2011. 'Heterosexy representation by young women on MySpace: The politics of performing an objectified self'. *Outskirts online journal*, 25(November). http://www.outskirts.arts.uwa.edu.au/volumes/volume-25/amy-shields-dobson.

Dobson, Amy Shields. 2018. 'Sexting, intimate and sexual media practices, and social justice'. In Dobson, Amy Shields, Brady Robards and Nicholas Carah (eds.), *Digital Intimate Publics and Social Media*. Basingstoke: Palgrave Macmillan, pp. 93–110.

Duggan, Lisa and Nan D. Hunter. 1996. *Sex wars: Sexual dissent and political culture*. New York: Routledge.

Dunn, Stephane. 2008. '"Baad Bitches" and Sassy Supermamas: Black Power Action Films'. Urbana: University of Illinois Press.

Durham, Meenakshi Gigi. 2010. *The Lolita Effect*. Woodstock: Overlook Press.

Duschinsky, Robbie. 2013. 'What does sexualisation mean?'. *Feminist Theory*, 14(3): 255–264.

Dworkin, Andrea. 1988. 'Against the Male Flood'. In her *Letters From a War Zone*. New York: Lawrence Hill Books.

Dworkin, Andrea. 1999. *Pornography; Men Possessing Women*. 2nd edition. New York and London: Plume (1st edition published in the UK in 1981 by the Women's Press, London).

Dworkin, Andrea. 2004. 'Pornography, prostitution, and a beautiful and tragic recent history'. In Stark, Christine and Rebecca Whisnant (eds.), *Not For Sale: feminists resisting prostitution and pornography*. Melbourne: Spinifex, pp. 137–145.

Dyer, Richard. 1993. *The Matter of Images: Essays on Representation*. London: Routledge.

Edgar, Eir-Anne. 2011. '"Xtravaganza!": drag representation and articulation in RuPaul's Drag Race'. *Studies in Popular Culture*, 34(1): 133–146.

Egan, R. Danielle. 2006. *Dancing for dollars and paying for love*. New York: Palgrave Macmillan.

Egan, R. Danielle. 2013. *Becoming sexual: A critical appraisal of the sexualization of girls*. Cambridge: Polity.

Ehrenreich, Barbara and Arlie Russell Hochschild (eds.). 2003. *Global woman: Nannies, maids, and sex workers in the new economy*. London: Granta Books.

Emerson, Rana A. 2002. '"Where My Girls At?": Negotiating Black Womanhood in Music Videos'. *Gender and Society*, 16(1): 115–135.

Evans, Adrienne and Sarah Riley. 2015. *Technologies of sexiness: Sex, identity, and consumer culture*. Oxford: Oxford University Press.

Evans, Judith. 1995. *Feminist Theory Today: An Introduction to second-wave feminism*, London: Sage (electronic version, unpaginated).

Fahs, Breanne and Sara I. McClelland. 2016. 'When sex and power collide: An argument for critical sexuality studies'. *Annual Review of Sex Research*, 53(4–5): 392–416.

Fateman, Johanna and Amy Scholder. 2019. *Last Days at Hot Slit: The Radical Feminism of Andrea Dworkin*. Cambridge, MA: MIT Press.

Fielding, Helen. 2003. 'Questioning Nature: Irigaray, Heidegger and the Potentiality of Matter'. *Continental Philosophy Review*, 36(3): 1–26.

Fight the New Drug. 2018. 'What's the Harm in Artificially Intelligent Sex Dolls? More than You Might Think'. https://fightthenewdrug.org/whats-the-harm-with-artificially-intelligent-sex-dolls/, accessed 27 August 2018.

Foubert, John D., Matthew W. Brosi and Sean R. Bannon. 2011. 'Pornography viewing among fraternity men: effect on bystander intervention, rape myth, acceptance and behavioral intent to commit sexual assault'. *Sexual Addiction & Compulsivity*, 18(4): 212–231.

Foucault, Michel. 1990. *History of Sexuality*, London: Penguin.

Fredrickson, Barbara L. and Kristen Harrison. 2005. 'Throwing like a girl: self-objectification predicts adolescent girls' motor performance'. *Journal of Sport and Social Issues*, 29(1): 79–101.

Fredrickson, Barbara L. and Tomi-Ann Roberts. 1997. 'Objectification theory: toward understanding women's lived experiences and mental health risks'. *Psychology of Women Quarterly*, 21: 173–206.

Fredrickson, Barbara L., Lee Meyerhoff Hendler, Stephanie Nilsen, Jean Fox O'Barr and Tomi-Ann Roberts. 2011. 'Bringing back the body: a retrospective on the development of objectification theory'. *Psychology of Women Quarterly*, 35(4): 689–696.

Freud, Sigmund. 2017 [1905]. *Three Essays on Sexuality* (James Strachey, trans). London: Verso.

Friday, Nancy. 1973. *My Secret Garden: Women's Sexual Fantasies*. New York: Pocket Editions.

Friday, Nancy. 1993. *Women on Top*, London: Arrow Books.

Friday, Nancy. 2009. *Beyond My Control: Forbidden Fantasies in an Uncensored Age*. Naperville, IL: Sourcebooks.

Fritz, Niki and Bryant Paul. 2017. 'From orgasms to spanking: a content analysis of the agentic and objectifying sexual scripts in feminist, for women and mainstream pornography'. *Sex Roles*, 77: 639–652. doi:10.1007/s11199-017-0759-6.

Gamson, Joshua. 1998. 'Publicity traps: Television talk shows and lesbian, gay, bisexual, and transgender visibility'. *Sexualities*, 1(1): 11–41.

Garland-Thomson, Rosemarie. 2009. *Staring: How we look*, Oxford, UK: Oxford University Press.

Garland-Thomson, Rosemarie. 1996. 'Introduction: From Wonder to Error – A Genealogy of Freak Discourse in Modernity'. In her edited collection *Cultural Spectacles of the Extraordinary Body*. New York: New York University Press, pp. 1–19.

Gill, Rosalind 2003. 'From Sexual Objectification to Sexual Subjectification: The Resexualisation of Women's Bodies in the Media'. *Feminist Media Studies*, 3(1): 100–106.

Gill, Rosalind. 2007a. *Gender and the Media*. London: Polity.

Gill, Rosalind, 2007b. 'Postfeminist media culture: Elements of a sensibility'. *European journal of cultural studies*, 10(2): 147–166.

Gill, Rosalind. 2008. 'Empowerment/sexism: Figuring female sexual agency in contemporary advertising'. *Feminism & Psychology*, 18: 35–60.

Gill, Rosalind. 2009. 'Beyond the "sexualization of culture" thesis: An intersectional analysis of "sixpacks","midriffs" and "hot lesbians" in advertising'. *Sexualities*, 12: 137–160.

Gill, Rosalind. 2017. 'The affective, cultural and psychic life of postfeminism: A postfeminist sensibility 10 years on'. *European Journal of Cultural Studies*, 20(6): 606–626. doi:10.1177/1367549417733003.

Gill, Rosalind and Shani Orgad. 2018. 'The shifting terrain of sex and power: From the "sexualization of culture" to "# MeToo"'. *Sexualities*, 21(8): 1313–1324.

Gledhill, Christine. 1978. 'Recent Developments in Feminist Criticism'. *Quarterly Review of Film Studies*, 3: 457–493.

Goldberg, Michelle. 2014. 'What is a Woman?'. *The New Yorker*. 4 August 2014. https://www.newyorker.com/magazine/2014/08/04/woman-2, accessed 28 February 2019.

Goldberg, Michelle. 2019. 'Not the Fun Kind of Feminist: How Trump Made Andrea Dworkin Relevant Again'. *The New York Times*. 22 February 2019. https://www.nytimes.com/2019/02/22/opinion/sunday/trump-feminism-andrea-dworkin.html, accessed 28 February 2019.

Gould, Jane. 1997. *Juggling: a memoir of work, family, and feminism*. New York: Feminist Press at the City University of New York.

Greenesmith, Heron. 2019. '"Feminist" Groups Teaming Up With Phyllis Schlafly's Organization to Put Trans Kids' Safety at Risk'. *Rewire.News*. 11 January 2019. https://rewire.news/article/2019/01/11/feminist-groups-teaming-up-with-phyllis-schlaflys-organization-to-put-trans-kids-safety-at-risk/, accessed 28 February 2020.

Greer, Germaine. 1970. *The Female Eunuch*. London: Paladin

Griffin, Susan. 1981. *Pornography and silence: Culture's revenge against nature*. New York: Harper & Row.

Griffith, James D., Sharon Mitchell, Christian L. Hart, Lea T. Adams and Lucy L. Gu. 2013. 'Pornography Actresses: An Assessment of the Damaged Goods Hypothesis'. *Journal of Sex Research*, 50(7): 621–632.

Grosz, Elizabeth. 2006. 'Naked'. In Smith, Marquard and Joanna Morra (ed.), *The Prosthetic Impulse: From Posthuman Present to a Biocultural Future*. Cambridge: MIT Press, pp. 187–202.

Haskell, Molly. 1974. *From Reverence to Rape: The Treatment of Women in Movies*. Chicago: University of Chicago Press.

Harrell, Zaje AT. 2002 'Trait self-objectification in college women's mental health: An examination of smokers and never-smokers'. PhD diss., University of Michigan.

Harvey, Laura and Jessica Ringrose. 2015. 'Sexting, ratings and (mis) recognition: teen boys performing classed and racialized masculinities in digitally networked publics'. In Renold, Emma, Jessica Ringrose and R. Danielle Egan (eds.), *Children, sexuality and sexualization*. London: Palgrave Macmillan, pp. 352–367.

Hasinoff, Amy Adele. 2013. 'Sexting as media production: Rethinking social media and sexuality'. *New Media & Society*, 15(4): 449–465.

Hasinoff, Amy Adele. 2015. *Sexting panic: Rethinking criminalization, privacy, and consent*. Urbana, IL: University of Illinois Press.

Haugen, Jason D. 2003. '"Unladylike Divas:" Language, Gender, and Female Gangsta Rappers'. *Popular Music and Society*, 26(4): 429–444.

Hendry, Natalie. 2014. 'Pics or it didn't happen*: mental health and visual practices'. https://tasayouth.wordpress.com/2014/04/10/pics-or-it-didnt-happen-mental-health-and-visual-practices/comment-page-1/, accessed 17 June 2019.

Hill Collins, Patricia. 2004. *Black sexual politics: African Americans, gender, and the new racism*. London and New York: Routledge.

Hill Collins, Patricia. 2008. 'Reply to Commentaries: Black Sexual Politics Revisited'. *Studies in Gender and Sexuality*, 9(1): 68–85. doi:10.1080/15240650701759292.

Hines, Sally. 2018. *Is Gender Fluid? A Primer for the 21st Century*. New York: Thames & Hudson.

Hines, Sally. 2019. 'The feminist frontier: on trans and feminism'. *Journal of Gender Studies*, 28(2): 145–157.

Hobson, Janell. 2018. *Venus in the dark: Blackness and beauty in popular culture*. Abingdon: Routledge.

hooks, bell. 1992. 'The Oppositional Gaze: Black Female Spectators'. In Bell, John (ed.), *Movies and Mass Culture*. New Brunswick: Rutgers University Press, pp. 247–264.

Horne, Sharon and Melanie J. Zimmer-Gembeck. 2005. 'Female sexual subjectivity and well-being: comparing late adolescents with different sexual experiences'. *Sexuality Research and Social Policy*, 2(3): 25–40.

Horne, Sharon and Melanie J. Zimmer-Gembeck. 2006. 'The Female Sexual Subjectivity Inventory: development and validation of a multidimensional invenstory for late adolescents and emerging adults'. *Psychology of Women Quarterly*, 30(2): 125–138.

Irigaray, Luce. 1974. *Speculum of the Other Woman*. New York: Cornell University Press.

Irigaray, Luce. 1985. *This Sex Which is Not One* (Catherine Porter with Carolyn Burke, trans.). Ithaca, NY: Cornell University Press.

Jacobs, Katrien. 2007. *Netporn: DIY web culture and sexual politics*. Plymouth, UK: Rowman & Littlefield.

Jaffe, Sarah. 2018. 'Why did a majority of white women vote for Trump?'. *New Labor Forum*, 27(1): 18–26.

Jeffreys, Sheila. 1990. *Anticlimax: a feminist perspective on the sexual revolution*. London: The Women's Press.

Jeffreys, Sheila. 1992. 'Introduction'. In Cole, Susan (ed.), *Pornography and the Sex Crisis*. Toronto: Second Story Press, pp. 13–16.

Jeffreys, Sheila. 1996. 'Return to Gender: Post-Modernism and Lesbianandgay Theory'. In Bell, Diane and Renate Klein (eds.), *Radically Speaking: Feminism Reclaimed*. Melbourne: Spinifex, pp. 359–374.

Jeffreys, Sheila. 2008. *The industrial vagina: The political economy of the global sex trade*. London: Routledge.

Jeffreys, Sheila. 2014. *Gender Hurts: A Feminist Analysis of Transgenderism*. New York: Routledge.

Jensen, Robert. 2007. *Getting Off: Pornography and the End of Masculinity*. Cambridge, MA: South End Press.

Johnston, Clare. 1973. 'Women's Cinema as Counter Cinema'. In Johnston, Clare (ed.), *Notes on Women's Cinema*. London: Society for Education in Film and Television, pp. 24–31.

Jones, Meredith. 2008. 'Media-bodies and screen-births: Cosmetic surgery reality television'. *Continuum*, 22(4): 515–524.

Jones, Meredith. 2013. 'Media-bodies and Photoshop'. In Attwood, Feona, Vince Campbell, I.Q. Hunter and Sharon Lockyer (eds.), *Controversial images: Media representations on the edge*. Basingstoke: Palgrave Macmillan, pp. 19–35.

Jones, Meredith. 2016. 'Je Suis Kim'. *Critical Studies in Fashion & Beauty*, 7(1): 129–140.

Jong, Erica. 1973. *Fear of Flying*. New York: Holt, Rinehart and Wilson.

Juffer, Jane. 1998. *At home with pornography: Women, sex, and everyday life*. New York: NYU Press.

Kagan, Dion. 2017. 'Representing queer sexualities'. In Smith, Clarissa and Feona Attwood with Brian McNair (eds.), *The Routledge Companion to Media, Sex and Sexuality*. London: Routledge, pp. 91–103.

Kaplan, E. Ann. 1997. *Looking for the Other: Feminism, Film and the Imperial Gaze*. London: Routledge.

Kappeler, Susanne. 1986. *The Pornography of Representation*. Minneapolis: University of Minnesota Press.

Kearney, Mary Celeste. 1997. 'The missing links: riot grrrl–feminism–lesbian culture'. In Whiteley, Sheila (ed.), *Sexing the Groove: Popular Music and Gender*. London and New York: Routledge, pp. 207–229.

Kempadoo, Kamala and Jo Doezema (eds.). 1998. *Global Sex Workers: Rights, Resistance, and Redefinition*. New York: Routledge.

Keyes, Cheryl. 2002. *Rap Music and Street Consciousness*. Urbana: University of Illinois Press.

Khazan, Olga. 2017. 'A Viral Short Story for the #MeToo Moment: The depiction of uncomfortable romance in "Cat Person" seems to resonate with countless women'. *The Atlantic*. 11 December 2017. https://www.theatlantic.com/technology/archive/2017/12/a-viral-short-story-for-the-metoo-moment/548009/, accessed 22 November 2018.

Khona, Rachel. 2016. 'Kim K, It's not "empowerment" if being sexy is all you're good at, Your Tango'. 10 March 2016. https://www.yourtango.com/2016286898/kim-kardashian-its-not-empowerment-if-being-sexy-all-youre-good-at, accessed 24 November 2019.

King is a Fink. 2010. 'Peep show – interview with Jiz Lee'. *Film Snobbery*. https://filmsnobbery.com/peep-show-interview-with-jiz-lee-part-one/, https://filmsnobbery.com/peep-show-interview-with-jiz-lee-part-two/, accessed 2 April 2019, archived at https://web.archive.org/web/20131104005120/http s://filmsnobbery.com/peep-show-interview-with-jiz-lee-part-one/ and http s://web.archive.org/web/20131104005010/https://filmsnobbery.com/peep-sho w-interview-with-jiz-lee-part-two/, accessed 4 May 2020.

Kingston, Drew. A. and Neil. M. Malamuth. 2011. 'Problems with aggregate data and the importance of individual differences in the study of pornography and sexual aggression: Comment on Diamond, Jozifkova, and Weiss (2010)'. *Archives of Sexual Behavior*. doi:10.1007/s10508-011-9743-3.

Kleiman, Kelly. 1999. 'Drag= blackface'. *Chicago-Kent Law Review*, 75: 669–686.

Klein, Melissa. 1997. 'Duality and Redefinition: young feminism and the alternative music community Third Wave Agenda'. In Heywood, Leslie and Jennifer Drake (eds.), *Third Wave Agenda: Being Feminist, Doing Feminism*. Minneapolis, MI: University of Minnesota Press, pp. 207–225.

Kohut, Taylor, Jodie Baer and Brendan Watts. 2016. 'Is pornography really about "Making hate to women?" Pornography users hold more gender egalitarian attitudes than nonusers in a representative American sample'. *Journal of Sex Research*, 53(1): 1–11.

Koivunen, Anu, Katriina Kyrölä and Ingrid Ryberg. 2018. 'Vulnerability as a political language'. In Anu Koivunen, Katriina Kyrölä and Ingrid Ryberg (eds.), *The power of vulnerability*. Manchester: Manchester University Press, pp. 1–26.

Krebs, Paula M. 1987. 'Lesbianism as a Political Strategy'. *Off Our Backs*. 17(6) (30 June): 17.

Kyrölä, Katariina. 2014. *The Weight of Images: Affect, Body Image and Fat in the Media*. Burlington: Ashgate.

Lamb, Sharon. 2010. 'Feminist ideals for a healthy female adolescent sexuality: a critique'. *Sex Roles*, 62(5–6): 294–306.

Lamb, Sharon and Zoë D. Peterson. 2012. 'Adolescent girls' sexual empowerment: two feminists explore the concept'. *Sex Roles*, 66: 703–712.

Langton, Rae. 2009. *Sexual Solipsism: Philosophical Essays on Pornography and Objectification*. Oxford: Oxford University Press.

Laqueur, Thomas. 2003. *Solitary Sex: A Cultural History of Masturbation*. New York: Zone Books.

Lauretis, de, Teresa. 1987. *Technologies of Gender: Essays on Theory, Film, and Fiction*. London: Macmillan.

Lee, Jiz. 2013. 'Uncategorized: genderqueer identity and performance in independent and mainstream porn'. In Taormino, Tristan, Celine Parreñas Shimizu, Constance Penley and Mireille Miller-Young (eds.), *The Feminist Porn Book*. New York: The Feminist Press at the City University of New York, pp. 273–278.

Lee, Jiz. 2015. 'How to come out like a porn star: an introduction'. In Lee, Jiz (ed.), *Coming Out Like a Porn Star: Essays on pornography, protection and privacy*. Berkeley: ThreeL Media (Kindle version, unpaginated).

Lee, Jiz. 2019. 'About Jiz Lee'. http://jizlee.com/bio/, accessed 1 April 2019.

Lee, Jiz and Rebecca Sullivan. 2016. 'Porn and labour: the labour of porn studies'. *Porn Studies*, 3(2): 104–106. doi:10.1080/23268743.2016.1184474.

Lee, Shayne. 2010. *Erotic revolutionaries: Black women, sexuality, and popular culture*. Hamilton Books: New York.

Lee, Taylor. 2004. 'In and out: a survivor's memoir of stripping'. In Stark, Christine and Rebecca Whisnant (eds.), *Not For Sale: feminists resisting prostitution and pornography*. Melbourne: Spinifex, pp. 56–63.

Levy, Ariel. 2005. *Female Chauvinist Pigs: Women and the Rise of Raunch Culture*. New York and London: Free Press.

Liebau, Carol Platt. 2007. *Prude: How the sex-obsessed culture damages girls (and America, too!)*. Nashville: FaithWords.

LeMaster, Benny. 2015. 'Discontents of being and becoming fabulous on RuPaul's drag u: Queer criticism in neoliberal times'. *Women's Studies in Communication*, 38(2): 167–186.

Lincoln, Sian and Brady Robards. 2016. 'Editing the project of the self: sustained Facebook use and growing up online'. *Journal of Youth Studies*, 20(4): 518–531.

Little, Simon. 2019. 'Feminist Speaker Deemed "Anti-Trans" by Critics Speaks at Vancouver Public Library'. *Global News. 11 January 2019.* https://globalnews.ca/news/4836690/feminist-speaker-anti-trans-vancou ver-public-library/, accessed 15 January 2019.

Livingstone, Sonia. 2008. 'Taking risky opportunities in youthful content creation: teenagers' use of social networking sites for intimacy, privacy and self-expression'. *New Media and Society*, 10(3): 393–411.

Losse, Kate. 2013. 'The Return of the Selfie'. *The New Yorker.* 5 June 2013. http://www.newyorker. com/tech/elements/the-return-of-the-selfie.html, accessed 29 January 2019.

MacKinnon, Catharine A. 1982. 'Feminism, Marxism, Method, and the State: An Agenda for Theory'. *Signs: Journal of women in culture and society*, 7(3): 515–544.

MacKinnnon, Catharine A. 1996. *Only Words*. Cambridge, MA: University of Harvard Press.

MacKinnon, Catherine A. and Andrea Dworkin (eds). 1998. *In Harm's Way: The Pornography Civil Rights Hearings*. Cambridge, MA: Harvard University Press.

Magubane, Zine. 2002 'Black Skins, Black Masks or "The Return of the White Negro" Race, Masculinity, and the Public Personas of Dennis Rodman and RuPaul'. *Men and Masculinities*, 4(3): 233–257.

Malamuth, Neil M. and Barry Spinner. 1980. 'A longitudinal content analysis of sexual violence in the best-selling erotic magazines'. *Journal of Sex Research*, 16: 226–237.

McCracken, Ellen. 1993. *Decoding Women's Magazines: From Mademoiselle to Ms*. Houndmills: Macmillan.

McDonald, Paul. 1997. 'Feeling and Fun: Romance, dance and the performing male body in the Take That videos'. In Whitely, Sheila (ed.), *Sexing the groove: Popular music and gender*. London and New York: Routledge, pp. 277–294.

McGahan, Michelle. 2015, 'Kim Kardashian feels good about "objectifying" herself in selfies & she should'. *Bustle.* 2 July 2015. https://www.bustle. com/articles/94259-kim-kardashian-feels-good-about-objectifyin g-herself-in-selfies-she-should, accessed 5 November 2019.

McKee, Alan. 2005. *The Public Sphere: an introduction*. Cambridge, UK: Cambridge University Press.

McKee, Alan. 2010. 'Everything is child abuse'. *Media International Australia*, 135(1): 131–140.

McKee, Alan. 2015. 'Methodological issues in defining aggression for content analyses of sexually explicit material'. *Archives of Sexual Behavior*, 44(1): 81–87.

McKee, Alan. 2016. 'Pornography as a creative industry: challenging the exceptionalist approach to pornography'. *Porn Studies*, 3(2): 107–119.

McKee, Alan, Catharine Lumby and Kath Albury. 2008. *The Porn Report*. Melbourne: Melbourne University Press.

McKee, Alan, Kath Albury, Michael Dunne, Sue Grieshaber, John Hartley, Catharine Lumby and Ben Mathews, 2010. 'Healthy Sexual Development: A Multidisciplinary Framework for Research'. *International Journal of Sexual Health*, 22(1): 14–19.

McKee, Alan, Sara Bragg and Tristan Taormino. 2015. 'Editorial introduction: entertainment media's evolving role in sex education'. *Sex Education*, 15(5): 451–457. doi:10.1080/14681811.2015.1071527.

McKee, Alan and Roger Ingham. 2018. 'Are there disciplinary differences in writing about pornography? A trialogue for two voices'. *Porn Studies*, 5 (1): 34–43.

McKinley, Nita Mary and Janet Shibley Hyde. 1996. 'The objectified body consciousness scale: development and validation'. *Psychology of Women Quarterly*, 20(2): 181–215.

McNair, Brian. 2002. *Striptease culture: Sex, media and the democratisation of desire*. London: Routledge.

McNair, Brian. 2013. *Porno? Chic!: How pornography changed the world and made it a better place*. London: Routledge.

McNally, James. 2016. 'Azealia Banks's "212": Black Female Identity and the White Gaze in Contemporary Hip-Hop'. *Journal of the Society for American Music*, 10(1): 54–81. doi:10.1017/S1752196315000541.

Mercer, John and Charlie Sarson. 2020. Fifteen seconds of fame: Rupaul's drag race, camp and 'memeability', Celebrity Studies, DOI: 10.1080/19392397.2020.1765102

Messaris, Paul. 2012. 'Visual "literacy" in the Digital Age'. *Review of Communication*, 12(2): 101–117.

Miller-Young, Mireille. 2010. 'Putting hypersexuality to work: Black women and illicit eroticism in pornography'. *Sexualities*, 13(2): 219–235. doi:10.1177/1363460709359229.

Milne, Carly (ed.), 2005. *Naked ambition: Women who are changing pornography*. Emeryville, CA: Seal Press.

Moi, Toril. 1985. *Sexual/Textual Politics: Feminist Literary Theory*. London: Routledge.

Mollard, Angela. 2016. 'It's time to get rid of the porn face and bring back the smile'. *news.com.au*. 21 November 2016. https://www.news.com.au/lifestyle/beauty/face-body/its-time-to-get-rid-of-porn-face-and-bring-ba ck-the-smile/news-story/316d651635ecf4368722d72e3d7d24ac, accessed 24 November 2019.

Mondin, Alessandra. 2014. 'Fair-trade porn + niche markets + feminist audience'. *Porn Studies*, 1(1–2): 189–192. doi:10.1080/23268743.2014.888251.

Monk-Turner, Elizabeth and H. Christine Purcell. 1999. 'Sexual violence in pornography: How prevalent is it?', *Gender Issues*, 17: 58–67.

Moore, Ramey. 2013. 'Everything Else Is Drag: Linguistic Drag and Gender Parody on RuPaul's Drag Race'. *Journal of Research in Gender Studies*, 3(2): 15–26.

Morgan, Robin. 1968. 'Letter from Robin Morgan to Richard S. Jackson, Mayor of Atlantic City'. 29 August 1968. *Duke University Library Digital Collections*. https://library.duke.edu/digitalcollections/wlmpc_maddc01002_maddc010020010/, accessed 16 January 2019.

Morgan, Robin. 1980. 'Theory and Practice: Pornography and Rape'. In Ledered, Laura (ed.), *Take Back the Night: Women on Pornography*. New York: William Morrow, pp. 134–140.

Morgan, Robin and Allison McNearney. 2018. 'I Was There: The 1968 Miss America Pageant Protest'. *History*. 7 September 2018. https://www.history.com/news/miss-america-protests-1968, accessed 16 January 2019.

Mulholland, Monique. 2013. *Young People and Pornography: Negotiating Pornification*. New York, NY: Palgrave.

Mulvey, Laura. 1975. 'Visual Pleasure and Narrative Cinema'. *Screen*, 16(3): 6–18.

Mulvey, Laura. 1981. 'Afterthoughts on "Visual Pleasure and Narrative Cinema" inspired by King Vidor's Duel in the Sun (1946)'. *Framework: The Journal of Cinema and Media*, (15/17): 12–15.

Mulvey, Laura. 2005. *Death 24x a Second*. London: Reaktion Books.

Murphy, Meghan. 2017. 'Sex robots epitomize patriarchy and offer men a solution to the threat of female independence'. *The Feminist Current*. 27 April 2017. https://www.feministcurrent.com/2017/04/27/sex-robots-epitomize-patriarchy-offer-men-solution-threat-female-independence/, accessed 16 January 2019.

Naezer, Marijke. 2018. 'Sexy selves: Girls, selfies and the performance of intersectional identities'. *European Journal of Women's Studies*: 1–16.

Nagle, Jill (ed.). 1997. *Whores and other Feminists*. New York and London: Routledge.

Namaste, Ki. 1996. 'Genderbashing: Sexuality, gender, and the regulation of public space'. *Environment and Planning D: Society and Space*, 14(2): 221–240.

New York Radical Women. 1970. 'No More Miss America!'. In Morgan, Robin (ed.), *Sisterhood is Powerful: An Anthology of Writings from the Women's Liberation Movement*. New York. Random House, pp. 584–588.

Nika, Colleen. 2012. 'Q&A: Azealia Banks on Why the C-Word is "Feminine"'. *Rolling Stone*. 10 September 2012. http://www.rollingstone.com/culture/culture-news/qa-azealia-banks-on-whythe-c-word-is-feminine-181176, accessed 24 June 2019.

Noll, Stephanie M. and Barbara L. Fredrickson. 1998. 'A mediational model linking self-objectification, body shame and disordered eating'. *Psychology of Women Quarterly*, 22: 623–636.

Nussbaum, Martha C. 1995. 'Objectification'. *Philosophy & Public Affairs*, 24(4): 249–291.

OBJECT!. 2019. 'Declaration of Women's Sex-Based Rights'. https://www.objectnow.org/womens-declaration/#more-122, accessed 28 April 2020.

O'Keefe, Theresa. 2016. 'Making feminist sense of no-platforming'. *Feminist Review*, 113(1): 85–92.

Oppliger, Patrice A. 2008. *Girls gone skank: The sexualization of girls in American culture*. Jefferson, NC: McFarland.

Orbach, Susie. 1978. *Fat is a Feminist Issue: The Anti-diet Guide to Permanent Weight Loss*. New York: Paddington Press.

Paasonen, Susanna. 2010. 'Labors of love: Netporn, Web 2.0, and the meanings of amateurism'. *New media and society*, 12(8): 1297–1312.

Paasonen, Susanna. 2018. 'Elusive Intensities, Fleeting Seductions, Affective Voices'. *Porn Studies*, 5(1): 27–33.

Paasonen, Susanna, Karina Nikunen and Laura Saarenmaa. 2007. 'Pornification and the education of desire'. In Paasonen, Susanna, Karina Nikunen and Laura Saarenmaa (eds.), *Pornification: Sex and Sexuality in Media Culture*. Oxford: Berg, pp. 1–20.

Paasonen, Susanna, Kylie Jarrett and Ben Light. 2019. *NSFW: Sex, Humor, and Risk in Social Media*. Cambridge, MA: MIT Press.

Papadopoulos, Linda and Home Office. 2010. 'Sexualisation of young people review'. London: Home Office. http://webarchive.nationalarchives.gov.uk/+/http:/www.homeoffice.gov.uk/documents/sexualisation-of-young-people.pdf, accessed 19 August 2019.

Patil, Vrushali. 2013. 'From Patriarchy to Intersectionality: A Transnational Feminist Assessment of How Far We've Really Come'. *Signs: Journal of Women in Culture and Society*, 38(4): 847–867.

Paul, Pamela. 2005. *Pornified: How Pornography is Transforming Our Lives, Our Relationships, and Our Families*. New York, NY: Times Books.

Pendleton, Eva. 1997. 'Love for Sale: Queering Heterosexuality'. In Nagle, Jill (ed.), *Whores and Other Feminists*. New York: Routledge, pp. 73–82.

Peter, Jochen and Patti M. Valkenburg. 2007. 'Adolescents' exposure to a sexualized media environment and their notions of women as sex objects'. *Sex roles*, 56(5–6): 381–395.

Phelan, Peggy. 1993. *Unmarked: The Politics of Performance*. London: Routledge.

Phipps, Alison, 2017. 'Sex Wars Revisited: a rhetorical economy of sex industry opposition'. *Journal of International Women's Studies*, 18(4): 306–320.

Pitkin, Hanna Fenichel. 1987. 'Rethinking reification'. *Theory and Society*, 16(2): 263–293.

Polhemus, Ted. 1994. *Streetstyle: From Sidewalk to Catwalk*. New York: Thames and Hudson.

Ponterotto, Diane. 2016. 'Resisting the Male Gaze: Feminist Responses to the 'Normatization' of the Female Body in Western Culture'. *Journal of International Women's Studies*, 17(1): 133–151.

Prosser, Jay. 1998. *Second skins: The body narratives of transsexuality*. New York: Columbia University Press.

Radway, Janice. 1984. *Reading the Romance: Women, Patriarchy, and Popular Fiction*. Chapel Hill: University of North Carolina Press.

Redstockings. n.d. 'The Miss America Protest: 1968'. https://www.red stockings.org/index.php/themissamericaprotest, accessed 16 July 2019.

Richardson, Niall. 2016. *Transgressive bodies: Representations in film and popular culture*. London: Routledge.

Richardson, Niall, Clarissa Smith and Angela Werndly. 2013. *Studying Sexualities: Theories, Representations, Cultures*. Basingstoke: Palgrave Macmillan.

Ringrose, Jessica. 2011. 'Are you sexy, flirty, or a slut? Exploring "sexualisation" and how teen girls perform/negotiate digital sexual identity on social networking sites'. In Gill, Rosalind and Christina Scharff (eds.), *New Femininities: Postfeminism, Neoliberalism and Subjectivity*. Basingstoke: Palgrave Macmillan, pp. 99–117.

Ringrose, Jessica and Emily Lawrence. 2018. 'Remixing misandry, manspreading, and dick pics: networked feminist humour on Tumblr'. *Feminist Media Studies*, 18(4): 686–704.

Rissel, Chris, Paul B. Badcock, A.M. Sheridan Smith, J. Richters, Richard O. de Visser, Andrew Grulich and Judy M. Simpson. 2014. 'Heterosexual experience and recent heterosexual encounters among Australian adults: the Second Australian Study of Health and Relationships'. *Sexual Health*, 11(5): 416–426. doi:10.1071/SH14105_CO.

Riviere, Joan. 1999. 'Womanliness as a Masquerade'. *Female Sexuality: Contemporary Engagements*, 8: 127–138.

Robbins, Ruth. 2000. *Literary Feminism*. London: Red Globe Press.

Rodowick, David. 1991. *The Difficulty of Difference: Psychoanalysis, Sexual Difference & Film Theory*. London: Routledge.

Rosen, Marjorie. 1973. *Popcorn Venus: Women, Movies, and the American Dream*. New York: Coward, McCann & Geoghegan.

Ruberg, Bonnie. 2016. 'Doing it for free: Digital labour and the fantasy of amateur online pornography'. *Porn Studies*, 3(2), pp. 147–159.

Rubin, Gayle. 1984. 'Thinking Sex: Notes for a Radical Theory of the Politics of Sexuality'. In Vance, Carole S. (ed.), *Pleasure and Danger: Exploring Female Sexuality*. London: Pandora, pp. 267–319.

Rubin, Gayle. 1995. 'Misguided, Dangerous and Wrong: An Analysis of Anti-Pornography Politics'. In Dines, Gail and Jean M. Humez (eds.), *Gender, Race and Class in Media: A Text-Reader*. Thousand Oaks: SAGE, pp. 244–253.

Rupp, Leila J., Verta Taylor and Eve Ilana Shapiro. 2010. 'Drag queens and drag kings: The difference gender makes'. *Sexualities*, 13(3): 275–294.

Rush, Emma and Andrea La Nauze. 2006. *Corporate paedophilia: Sexualisation of children in Australia*. Canberra: The Australia Institute.

Russo, Anne. 1998. 'Feminists confront pornography's subordinating practices: policies and strategies for change'. In Dines, Gail, Robert Jensen and Anne Russo (eds.), *Pornography: the production and consumption of inequality*. New York and London: Routledge, pp. 9–35.

Sanders, Teela. 2005. '"It's just acting": sex workers' strategies for capitalizing on sexuality'. *Gender, Work & Organization*, 12(4): 319–342.

Sarracino, Carmine and Kevin M. Scott. 2008. *The Porning of America: The Rise of Porn Culture, What It Means, and Where We Go from Here*. Boston, MA: Beacon Press.

Saul, Jennifer M. 2006. 'On treating things as people: objectification, pornography, and the history of the vibrator'. *Hypatia*, 21(2): 45–61.

Schorn, Johanna. 2012. 'Subverting pornormativity: feminist and queer interventions'. *Gender Forum: an Internet journal for gender studies*, (37): 15–24.

Scolari, Rosalie. 2010. 'Genderqueer feminist porn star: Jiz Lee'. *The Scavenger*. http://www.thescavenger.net/sex-gender-sexuality-diversity-archived/65-queer/393-genderqueer-feminist-porn-star-jiz-lee-74398.html, accessed 2 April 2019.

Scott, Joseph. E. and Stephen J. Cuvelier. 1993. 'Violence and sexual violence in pornography: Is it really increasing?', *Archives of Sexual Behavior*, 22: 357–371.

Sedgwick, Eve Kosofsky. 2003. *Touching Feeling: Affect, Pedagogy, Performativity*. Durham, NC: Duke University Press.

Sedgwick, Eve Kosofsky and Adam Frank. 1995. 'Shame in the Cybernetic Fold: Reading Silvan Tomkins'. In Kosofsky Sedgwick, Eve and Adam Frank (eds.), *Shame and Its Sisters: A Silvan Tomkins Reader*. Durham: Duke University Press, pp. 1–28.

See, Jane. 2019a. 'Historic Gender Parity in Children's Television'. The Geena Davis Institute on Gender in Media. https://seejane.org/wp-con tent/uploads/see-jane-2019-full-report.pdf, accessed 19 June 2019.

See, Jane. 2019b. 'The Geena Benchmark Report: 2007–2017'. The Geena Davis Institute on Gender in Media. https://seejane.org/wp-content/uploa ds/geena-benchmark-report-2007-2017-2-12-19.pdf, accessed 19 June 2019.

Segal, Lynne. 1992. 'Introduction'. In Segal, Lynne and Mary McIntosh (eds.), *Sex Exposed: Sexuality and the Pornography Debate*. London: Virago: pp. 1–11.

Segal, Lynne. 1993. 'False promises: anti-pornography feminism'. *Socialist Register*, 29: 92–105.

Segal, Lynne. 2010. 'Feminism did not fail'. https://www.radicalphilosophy. com/commentary/feminism-did-not-fail, accessed 15 April 2019.

Sedgwick, Eve Kosofsky. 2003. *Touching Feeling: Affect, Pedagogy, Perfor-mativity*. Durham: Duke University Press.

Serano, Julia. 2016. *Whipping girl: A transsexual woman on sexism and the scapegoating of femininity*. London: Hachette UK.

Setty, Emily. 2018. 'Sexting ethics in youth digital cultures: risk, shame and the negotiation of privacy and consent'. PhD diss., University of Surrey.

Shor, Eran and Golshan Golriz. 2019. 'Gender, race, and aggression in mainstream pornography'. *Archives of Sexual Behaviour*, 48(3): 739–751.

Silver, Anna Krugovoy. 2004. *Victorian Literature and the Anorexic Body*. Cambridge, UK: Cambridge University Press.

Simon, William and John H. Gagnon. 1986. 'Sexual Scripts: Permanence and Change'. *Archives of Sexual Behavior*, 15(2): 97–120.

Simonton, Ann and Carol Smith. 2004. 'Who are women in pornography?'. In Stark, Christine and Rebecca Whisnant (eds.), *Not For Sale: feminists resisting prostitution and pornography*. Melbourne: Spinifex, pp. 352–361.

Smith, Anna Marie. 1993. '"What is Pornography?": An Analysis of the Policy Statement of the Campaign against Pornography and Censorship'. *Feminist Review*, 43(1): 71–87.

Smith, Clarissa. 2010. 'Pornographication: A discourse for all seasons'. *International Journal of Media & Cultural Politics*, 6(1): 103–108.

Smith, Clarissa. 2012. 'Reel intercourse: Doing sex on camera'. In Hines, Claire and Darren Kerr (eds.), *Hard to swallow: Hard-core pornography on screen*. London: Wallflower Press, pp. 194–214.

Smith, Clarissa and Feona Attwood. 2013. 'Emotional Truths and Thrilling Side Shows: The Resurgence of Anti-Porn Feminism'. In Taormino, Tri-stan, Celine Parrenas Shimizu, Constance Penley and Mireille Miller-Young (eds.), *The Feminist Porn Book: The Politics of Producing Pleasure*. New York: Feminist Press at the City University of New York, pp. 41–57.

Smith, Molly and Juno Mac. 2018. *Revolting Prostitutes: The Fight for Sex Workers' Rights*. London: Verso.

Sommers-Flanagan, Rita, John Sommers-Flanagan and Britta Davis. 1993. 'What's happening on Music Television?; a gender role content analysis'. *Sex Roles*, 28(11–12): 745–753.

Spišák, Sanna. 2016. '"Everywhere they say that it's harmful but they don't say how, so I'm asking here": young people, pornography and negotiations with notions of risk and harm'. *Sex Education*, 16(2): 130–142.

Spitzack, Carole. 1990. *Confessing Excess: women and the politics of body reduction*. New York: State University Press of New York.

Sprinkle, Annie M. 1999. 'The forty reasons why whores are my heroes'. *Social Alternatives*, 18(3): 8.

Stanko, Elizabeth A. 2001. 'Violence'. In McLaughlin, Eugene and John Muncie (eds.), *The Sage Dictionary of Criminology*. London: Sage, pp. 315–318.

Stardust, Zahra. 2014. '"Fisting is not permitted": criminal intimacies, queersexualities and feminist porn in the Australian legal context'. *Porn Studies*, 1(3): 242–259.

Stark, Christine. 2004. 'Girls to boyz: sex radical women promoting pornography and prostitution'. In Stark, Christine and Rebecca Whisnant (eds.), *Not For Sale: feminists resisting prostitution and pornography*. Melbourne: Spinifex, pp. 278–291.

Stein, Arlene. 2006. *Shameless: Sexual Dissidence in American Culture*. New York: New York University Press.

Stoller, Robert J. 1968. *Sex and gender: Vol. 1. The development of masculinity and femininity*. New York: Science House.

Stone, Sandy. 1991. 'The Empire Strikes Back: A Posttranssexual Manifesto'. In Straub, Kristina and Julia Epstein (eds.), *Body Guards: The Cultural Politics of Gender Ambiguity*. New York: Routledge, pp. 280–304.

Strings, Sabrina and Long T. Bui. 2014. '"She Is Not Acting, She Is" The conflict between gender and racial realness on RuPaul's Drag Race'. *Feminist Media Studies*, 14(5): 822–836.

Stryker, Susan. 2006. '(De)subjugated knowledge: an introduction to transgender studies'. In Stryker, Susan and Simon Whittle (eds.), *The Transgender Studies Reader*. New York and Abingdon: Routledge, pp. 1–17.

Stryker, Susan and Simon Whittle (eds.). 2006. *The Transgender Studies Reader*. New York and Abingdon: Routledge.

Studlar, Gaylyn. 1984. 'Masochism and the Perverse Pleasures of the Cinema'. *Quarterly Review of Film Studies*, 9(4): 267–282.

Sundén, Jenny and Susanna Paasonen. 2019. 'Inappropriate laughter: Affective homophily and the unlikely comedy of #MeToo'. *Social Media + Society*, 5(4): 1–10.

Taormino, Tristan, Celine Parreñas Shimizu, Constance Penley and Mireille Miller-Young (eds.). 2013. *The Feminist Porn Book*. New York: The Feminist Press at the City University of New York.

Tate, Shirley. 2012. 'Michelle Obama's arms: Race, respectability, and class privilege'. *Comparative American Studies An International Journal*, 10 (2–3): 226–238.

Thompson, Denise. 2001. *Radical Feminism Today*. London, Thousand Oaks and New Delhi: Sage Publications.

Tiidenberg, Katrin. 2018. *Selfies: Why we love (and hate) them*. Bingley: Emerald.

Tiidenberg, Katrin and Edgar Gómez Cruz. 2015. 'Selfies, image and the re-making of the body'. *Body & society*, 21(4): 77–102.

Tolman, Deborah L. 2012. 'Female adolescents, sexual empowerment and desire: a missing discourse of gender inequity'. *Sex Roles*, 66 (11–12): 746–757. doi:10.1007/s11199-012-0122-x.

Tramontana, Mary Katharine. 2015. 'Gender Fuck'. *The New Inquiry*. https://thenewinquiry.com/gender-fuck/, accessed 2 April 2019.

Tuck, Greg. 2009. 'The Mainstreaming of Masturbation: Autoeroticism and Consumer Capitalism'. In Attwood, Feona (ed.), *Mainstreaming Sex: The Sexualization of Wester Culture*. London: IB Tauris, pp. 77–92.

Tucker, Lauren R. 1998. 'The framing of Calvin Klein: A frame analysis of media discourse about the August 1995 Calvin Klein Jeans advertising campaign'. *Critical Studies in Media and Communication*, 15(2): 141–157.

Vance, Carole S. 1984a. 'Pleasure and danger: towards a politics of sexuality'. In Vance, Carole S. (ed.), *Pleasure and Danger: Exploring Female Sexuality*. London: Pandora, pp. 1–27.

Vance, Carole S. (ed). 1984b. *Pleasure and Danger: Exploring Female Sexuality*. London: Pandora.

Vance, Carole S. 1997. 'Negotiating Sex and Gender in the Attorney General's Commission on Pornography'. In Lancaster, Roger N. and Micaela di Leonardo (eds.), *The gender/sexuality reader: Culture, history, political economy*. New York: Routledge, pp. 440–452.

Vendemia, Megan A. and David C. DeAndrea. 2018. 'The effects of viewing thin, sexualized selfies on Instagram: Investigating the role of image source and awareness of photo editing practices'. *Body image*, 27: 118–127.

Waite, Catherine. 2011. 'Sociality Online: An Exploratory Study into the Online Habits of Young Australians'. *Youth Studies Australia*, 30(4): 17–24.

Walby, Sylvia. 1989. 'Theorising Patriarchy'. *Sociology*, 23(2): 213–234.

Wald, Elijah, 2015. 'Cocksucker Blues: A Respectful Exploration of Cunnilingus in African American Popular Song'. Paper presented at the EMP Pop Conference. Seattle, WA. 17 April 2015. http://www.empmuseum.

org/programs-plus-education/programs/pop-conference.aspx?t=zwald-e# Tabs, accessed 8 October 2015.

Walker, Melissa. 2013. 'The Good, the Bad, and the Unexpected Consequences of Selfie Obsession', *Teen Vogue*. 6 August 2013. https://www.teenvogue.com/story/selfie-obsession, accessed 15 September 2019.

Webber, Valerie and Rebecca Sullivan. 2018. 'Constructing a crisis: porn panics and public health'. *Porn Studies*, 5(2): 192–196.

Weeks, Kathi. 2011. *The Problem with Work: Feminism, Marxism, Antiwork Politics, and Postwork Imaginaries.* Durham: Duke University Press.

Weiss, Suzannah, 2017. '5 Negative effects of objectifying women, according to science'. *Bustle.* 13 December 2017. https://www.bustle.com/p/5-negative-effects-of-objectifying-women-according-to-science-2959186, accessed 17 November 2019.

Weitzer, Ronald. 2010. 'The movement to criminalize sex work in the United States'. *Journal of Law and Society*, 37(1): 61–84.

Whisnant, Rebecca. 2004. 'Confronting pornography: some conceptual basics'. In Stark, Christine and Rebecca Whisnant (eds.), *Not For Sale: feminists resisting prostitution and pornography.* Melbourne: Spinifex, pp. 15–27.

Whisnant, Rebecca and Christine Stark. 2004. 'Introduction'. In Stark, Christine and Rebecca Whisnant (eds.), *Not For Sale: feminists resisting prostitution and pornography.* Melbourne: Spinifex, pp. xi–xvii.

White, Theresa Renee. 2013. 'Missy "Misdemeanor" Elliott and Nicki Minaj: Fashionistin' Black Female Sexuality in Hip-Hop Culture – Girl Power or Overpowered?'. *Journal of Black Studies*, 44(6): 607–626.

Whittle, Simon. 2006. 'Foreword'. In Stryker, Susan and Simon Whittle (eds.), *The Transgender Studies Reader.* New York and Abingdon: Routledge, pp. xi–xv.

Wilkinson, Sue and Celia Kitzinger. 1996. 'The Queer Backlash'. In Bell, Diane and Renate Klein (eds.), *Radically Speaking: Feminism Reclaimed.* Melbourne: Spinifex, pp. 375–382.

Williams, Cristan. 2016. 'Radical inclusion: Recounting the trans inclusive history of radical feminism'. *Transgender Studies Quarterly*, 3(1–2): 254–258.

Williamson, Judith. 2006. 'A Piece of the Action: Images of "Woman" in the Photography of Cindy Sherman'. In Burton, Johanna (ed.), *Cindy Sherman.* Cambridge, MA: MIT Press, pp. 39–52.

Wolf, Naomi. 1991. *The Beauty Myth: how images of beauty are used against women.* New York: Anchor Press.

Wolkowitz, Carol, Rachel Lara Cohen, Teela Sanders and Kate Hardy (eds.). 2013. *Body/sex/work: intimate, embodied and sexualised labour.* Basingstoke: Macmillan International Higher Education.

Yancy, George. 2008. 'Colonial Gazing: The Production of the Body as "Other"'. *Western Journal of Black Studies*, 32(1): 1–15.

Zappavigna, Michele. 2016. 'Social media photography: construing subjectivity in Instagram images'. *Visual Communication*, 15(3): 271–292.

~~Zelizer, Viviana. 2005. *The Purchase of Intimacy*. Princeton, NJ: Princeton~~ University Press.

Zimmerman, Amanda and John Dahlberg. 2008. 'The Sexual Objectification of Women in Advertising: A Contemporary Cultural Perspective'. *Journal of Advertising Research*, 48(1): 71–79.

Zurbriggen, Eileen L., Rebecca L. Collins, Sharon Lamb, Tomi-Ann Roberts, Deborah L. Tolman, L. Monique Ward and Jeanne Blake. 2010. *Report of the APA Task Force on the Sexualization of Girls*. 2nd edition. Washington: American Psychological Association.

Index